DREAMS OF HEALING

Transforming Nightmares
into Visions of Hope

DREAMS OF HEALING

Transforming Nightmares
into Visions of Hope

Kelly Bulkeley

PAULIST PRESS
New York/Mahwah, N.J.

Cover design by Trudi Gershenov Design

Book design by Lynn Else

Library of Congress Cataloging-in-Publication Data

Bulkeley, Kelly, 1962-
    Dreams of healing : transforming nightmares into visions of hope / Kelly Bulkeley.
       p. cm.
    Includes bibliographical references and index.
    ISBN 0-8091-4153-1 (alk. paper)
    1. Nightmares. 2. Dreams. 3. Dream interpretation. 4. Disasters—Psychological aspects. 5. Crisis intervention (Mental health services) 6. Counseling. I. Title.
    BF1099.N53 B85 2003
    155.9′35—dc21

                            2003001687

Published by Paulist Press
997 Macarthur Boulevard
Mahwah, New Jersey 07430

www.paulistpress.com

Printed and bound in the
United States of America

Contents

For My Parents

Acknowledgments

This book started, as so many do, with a conversation. Chris Bellitto of Paulist Press listened to my initial ideas about dreams, nightmares, and caregiving in the aftermath of September 11, and he gave me the critical feedback I needed to develop those passionate but inchoate ideas into a book that is addressed to a much wider audience than I originally had in mind. I cannot speak for all writers, but I know that for me the relationship with an editor always has an element of tension to it, and I appreciate the way Chris skillfully managed that tension and helped to steer my authorial narcissism ("What? You mean everything I've written isn't absolutely brilliant and perfect just the way it is?") in creative and productive directions. I also thank Chris for putting me in touch with his wife, Karen Bellitto, a social worker at Calvary Hospital in Bronx, New York, who provided me with some wonderful insights about clinical work with people suffering major life crises.

Many, many other personal conversations have inspired and guided me in the writing of this book, and I want to express my gratitude to the following people for sharing their experiences and perspectives with me: Gloria Sturzenacker, Stanley Krippner, the Reverend Jeremy Taylor, Richard Wilkerson, Nancy Grace, Phil King, Charles McPhee, Kathleen Sullivan, Alan Siegel, Bill Domhoff, Jacqueline Luck, Roger Knudson, Jane White-Lewis, Cynthia Pearson, Anne Frey, Franz Metcalf, Tracey Kahan, Sara Ridberg, Trisha Chang, Deirdre Barrett, Ernest Hartmann, Lewis Rambo, Patricia Garfield, Tom Campbell, and the Reverend Dan Coughlin. Thanks are due as well to the many people who gave permission to include their dreams in this book (with names and other identifying details removed). I also benefited from several public gatherings in which I learned valuable information that became part of this book. These gatherings were sponsored by the Graduate Theological Union; the Person, Culture, and Religion Group of the American Academy of Religion; and the Association for the Study of Dreams. I hope I have faithfully recounted the many wise comments I heard from the participants at those meetings.

The members of my immediate family—Hilary, Dylan, Maya, and Conor—were as supportive as ever during the writing of *Dreams of Healing*. I can never give enough thanks for their love and encouragement. In the weeks and months following September 11, the subject of my writing was also the subject of many family discussions at the dinner table, and in a very real sense every one of my family members contributed to what is contained in the following pages.

One of the people with whom I spoke while doing research for this project described a dream she had a week after September 11. In the dream she is sitting in a room, like at a retreat center, with several other people. They are all connected to each other by wires or electrical cords that create a network among them. My friend said she understood the dream as an expression of her need for connection and regained power to counter the shock and helplessness she and so many others felt after the terrorist attack. I love this image of an "energy network" that helps to renew personal connections in a time of crisis—it's a perfect illustration of the dynamic conversational process that generated the content of this book, and it beautifully highlights the book's ultimate goal: to show how dreams can lead us through the despair and confusion of unexpected catastrophe to the development of new capacities for vitality, creativity, and relationship.

Introduction

The emotional shock waves from the events of September 11, 2001, are still reverberating throughout American society. Beyond the astonishing loss of life and the incredible property damage incurred, the intense feelings of horror and shock so many people experienced that day have deeply wounded the national psyche. The audacity of the attack, its overwhelming destructiveness, the magnitude of its damaging effects throughout the country, and the horrifying drama of its live media coverage all combined to produce one of the worst national disasters in American history. It is hard to think of any other single event that struck the country with such sudden, painful emotional force and in such an immediate and widespread fashion.

However, as historically unique as it undoubtedly was, September 11 does share characteristics with other kinds of unexpected crisis and disaster. The psychologically damaging effects of September 11 reflect many of the same features that can be observed whenever people suffer a terrible tragedy. One of the most common of these features is an upsurge of vivid dreams and nightmares. People are often puzzled and even frightened by these strange dream experiences, but psychologists have long known that such dreams play a vital role in the process of recovering from and responding creatively to crises, conflicts, and disasters.[1] We do not yet fully understand all the psychological functions of dreaming, but we do know that foremost among them is the function of *meaning-making*. When we go to sleep at night our minds do not simply shut off, to be turned back on when we wake up in the morning. On the contrary, our minds remain active throughout the sleep cycle, working vigorously at the task of processing new information from our daily lives, weaving together perceptions, experiences, memories, and desires in order to sustain and enhance our ongoing sense of self and world.[2] When something like September 11 happens that is totally unexpected and intensely frightening, we call the effect "traumatizing," and in such situations the dreaming mind makes extraordinary efforts to achieve its primary goal of meaning-making. Whether the trauma is individual (a car accident, illness, criminal assault) or collective (an earthquake, flood, assassination, terrorist attack), the vital function of dreaming is always the same: to express the turbulent emotions, work through the confusion, heal the psychic wounds, and creatively envision new possibilities for meaning and order in the world.

This book is addressed to two main audiences. The first consists of people who have been deeply affected by some kind of crisis or trauma, who have experienced strange and disturbing dreams themselves, and who are looking for insight into what their dreams might mean. The second audience consists of people working in a caregiving capacity—as therapists, counselors, clergy, physicians, educators, and parents—who want to learn how dreams and nightmares can help them in their efforts to relieve other people's suffering. Although many of the dreams in the book relate to the events of September 11, I also discuss dreams in relation to many other kinds of sudden disaster, and I offer suggestions about various ways that dreams can be a valuable resource in virtually every form of caregiving practice. Starting in chapter 1, I introduce readers to "Nan," a fifty-seven-year-old woman who was critically injured in a car accident in the fall of 2001 and who shared with me the dreams and nightmares she experienced in the six months following the accident. We return to Nan's story at several points in the book to discuss the striking images, recurrent themes, and surprising transformations in her dreaming experience. Nan's dream series provides a relatively personal, small-scale portrait of the healing process, which I hope will balance and complement the larger-scale portrait drawn from people's dreams and nightmares following September 11. Whether a disaster harms millions of people or just one, the healing powers of dreaming respond to the crisis in the same basic way, by mobilizing the tremendously creative meaning-making capacities of the human psyche.

Let me say a few words about my background and my approach to dreams. My academic training is in the field of religion and psychology, and I chose that interdisciplinary field when I started graduate school because I felt it offered the best means of studying the multiple dimensions of dreaming experience. Religious traditions throughout history have regarded dreams as powerfully revelatory experiences, and those traditions contain much wisdom about the potential of dreams to heal, guide, and transform people's lives. Modern psychological research has taught us a great deal about the formation and function of dreams, and by combining that research with the traditional religious insights I believe we are best able to recognize and appreciate the place of dreaming in human life.

Many people, when they hear the term "dream interpretation," think immediately of the theories of Sigmund Freud and Carl Jung. I should say, then, that I do not consider myself a "Freudian" or a "Jungian" in the sense of slavishly following their interpretive methods. I definitely do use many of their ideas, but I also draw on the work of cognitive neuroscientists, developmental psychologists, cultural anthropologists, and historians of religion. I see dreaming as a dynamic interaction of physiological, psychological, cultural, and spiritual forces, and I am skeptical toward any theory that claims to have found a single, all-purpose answer to the question of what dreams mean. There is an irreducible, inexhaustible mystery to dreaming, and although we may discover valuable insights in our dreams, we will never definitively capture or confine them within the boundaries of a single conceptual framework. Dreaming is as infinitely creative as life itself, and just as resistant to strictly rational accounting and explanation.

In trying to understand what a particular dream might mean, I start by focusing on the details of the dreamer's experience: the emotions and sensations felt within the dream, the characters, colors, and settings that appear, the most vivid images, the most striking impressions. I look for what the given dream has in common with other dreams, and I also look for what is unusual and exceptional about this dream (that is, those "bizarre" elements that make dreams so baffling and yet so intriguing). I believe every dream is absolutely unique, like a fingerprint or a snowflake, and thus to understand a dream's meaning we have to recognize and appreciate its distinct individuality, even as we try to discern themes and patterns it has in common with other dreams.

Dreams are always rooted in the personal life of the dreamer, so attention must be given to the current life circumstances of the dreamer, including his or her personality characteristics, family life, physical health, romantic relationships, and so on. The same dream image can mean very different things to different people, depending on their backgrounds and personalities. A dream of a big rainstorm might mean one thing to a person going through a divorce, another to a farmer in a drought-stricken region, another to a young child who's afraid of thunder, another to a person who's clinically depressed, and another to a woman who's nine months pregnant. There is no "one size fits all" definition for any dream image because every dream bears the unique stamp of the dreamer's life and personality.

The effort to interpret and understand dreams is not equivalent to solving a mathematical equation, in which a single, unambiguous result is produced at the end of the process. Dream interpretation is much more comparable to art or literary criticism, in which close, detailed analysis is combined with empathetic intuition and creative imagination. My fundamental premise is that there is no single correct meaning to any dream; there are many possible interpretations, some of which are more valid than others. The only way to tell if an interpretation is a good one is by a process of careful questioning, testing, and reflecting. I use the following four principles to guide this process:[3]

1. *The dreamer knows best what his or her dream means.* Only the dreamer has direct access to all the images and feelings in the dream, and only the dreamer is familiar with all the memories and associations making up the dream's broader context. This does not necessarily imply the dreamer's own view on the dream is the only legitimate one; dreamers are often unaware of many significant dimensions of their dreams (as Freud noted). But this principle does mean that the dreamer's perspective must be accounted for in any valid interpretation. It further suggests that interpreters should be concerned if their claims about a dream's meaning deviate too far from what the dreamer feels the dream means.

2. *A good interpretation will account for as many of the dream's details as possible.* I call this the "principle of internal coherence." An interpretation that brings together more of the various elements of a dream will be better than an interpretation that refers only to a few isolated pieces. Naturally, problems arise if interpreters try to force all the details of a dream into a single fixed idea. But on the whole, the interpretation that accounts for the most details of the dream is the best interpretation.

3. *A good interpretation will make as many connections as possible between the dream's content and the dreamer's waking life.* This is the "principle of external coherence," and it is grounded

in the fact that dreams are usually created out of images, ideas, and feelings from the dreamer's daily existence. A good interpretation identifies the connections between those waking life sources and the various symbolic strands of the dream. Sometimes the connections relate to experiences from the previous day; sometimes they involve events from farther in the past; and sometimes they refer to anticipated events in the future. The principle of external coherence asks how well any proposed interpretation has contextualized the given dream in the full temporal span of the dreamer's life and how well it accounts for the waking-world origins of the dream's imagery.

4. *A good interpretation will be open to new and surprising discoveries and will look beyond the obvious (what is already known) to find the novel and the unexpected (what is not already known).* The biggest difficulty in understanding dreams is avoiding the trap of our own biases and expectations. It is frightfully easy to see what you want to see and find what you want to find when interpreting a dream. The best way to overcome this propensity to self-deception is to start the process by admitting that we do not know where the interpretive process will lead. We try as hard as we can to stay open to the possibility that new meanings will emerge, and we critically question our own assumptions every step of the way. On this point I share the view of Jung when he said, "So difficult is it to understand a dream that for a long time I have made it a rule, when someone tells me a dream and asks for my opinion, to say first of all to myself: 'I have no idea what this dream means.' After that I can begin to examine the dream."[4]

These four principles offer a good starting point for efforts to understand what particular dreams might mean. In the pages that follow I use these principles to guide my discussion of the various types of dreams people have had in response to crises and traumas. As the book proceeds I hope readers will begin developing their own ideas about what the dreams mean, and I actively encourage you in this process—the more you engage your critical skills and intuitive sensitivities, the better able you will be to make sense of your own dreams and the dreams of others.

Essential Bibliography

Barrett, Deirdre, ed. 1996. *Trauma and Dreams.* Cambridge: Harvard University Press.

Bulkeley, Kelly. 1997. *An Introduction to the Psychology of Dreaming.* Westport: Praeger.

———. 2001b. Penelope as Dreamer: The Perils of Interpretation. In *Dreams: A Reader on the Religious, Cultural, and Psychological Dimensions of Dreaming,* ed. K. Bulkeley. New York: Palgrave.

Cartwright, Rosalind. 1991. Dreams That Work: The Relation of Dream Incorporation to Adaptation of Stressful Events. *Dreaming* 1 (1):3–10.

Hartmann, Ernest. 1998. *Dreams and Nightmares: The New Theory on the Origin and Meaning of Dreams.* New York: Plenum.

Jung, C. G. 1975. On the Nature of Dreams. In *Dreams.* Original ed., 1948. Princeton: Princeton University Press.

Notes

1. Good sources of information are Barrett 1996, Hartmann 1998, and Cartwright 1991.
2. For more information about psychological theories about dreams, see *An Introduction to the Psychology of Dreaming* (Bulkeley 1997). Although I speak here of "the dreaming mind," it is clear that dreams involve the dynamic activation of many neurological structures of the brain, so I will also be

using the more accurate, if less elegant, term "brain-mind system" to describe the psychophysiological origins of dream experience.

3. I discuss these same principles at greater length in "Penelope as Dreamer: The Perils of Interpretation" (Bulkeley 2001b).

4. Jung 1975, 69.

1. Post-Traumatic Stress and Nightmares

The PTSD Diagnosis

A woman who lived in an apartment a block away from the World Trade Center had recurrent nightmares for many nights after September 11 of not being able to find her children, and in one dream she found herself in the cockpit of a huge jet, fighting with hijackers: "Clouds are coming at me, fast. The plane is going down. I am bracing myself, waiting for the impact."[1]

After eight hours of surgery to repair the broken vertebrae in her neck following the car accident, a woman was placed in a hospital bed surrounded by a curtain, where over the next several nights she was plagued by bad dreams: "Horrible nightmares of the damask curtain transforming to creatures like demons from Hell threatening me. I was so afraid I couldn't close my eyes with night after night of sheer terror!"[2]

Anyone familiar with post-traumatic stress disorder (PTSD) will recognize in such cases one of the malady's most typical symptoms: terrible dreams and nightmares that deeply disrupt the capacity to have a normal, restful sleep. PTSD as a clinical diagnosis is a fairly recent addition to psychiatric theory and practice. It was added in 1980 to the American Psychiatric Association's *Diagnostic and Statistical Manual of Mental Disorders* (DSM-III) in recognition of the distinctly destructive psychological impact of events outside the normal range of human experience. According to Matthew Friedman, Executive Director of the National Center for PTSD, the clinicians who initially formulated the

1

PTSD diagnosis "considered traumatic events as clearly different from the very painful stressors that constitute the normal vicissitudes of life such as divorce, failure, rejection, serious illness, financial reverses, and the like....This dichotomization between traumatic and other stressors was based on the assumption that although most individuals have the ability to cope with ordinary stress, their adaptive capacities are likely to be overwhelmed when confronted by a traumatic stressor."[3]

Much of the early research on PTSD focused on the horrifying experiences of Vietnam War veterans. Although the veterans of previous wars had clearly suffered severe psychological problems ("disordered action of the heart" in the Civil War, "shell shock" in World War I, "combat fatigue" in World War II[4]), Vietnam veterans presented clinicians with especially acute forms of war-related emotional distress. The unpredictable guerilla tactics of the Viet Cong, the agonizing difficulty of distinguishing civilians from combatants, and the bitter controversy back home in America about the moral justification for the war all combined to make military service in Vietnam an extremely damaging psychological experience, with painful and long-lasting consequences. The National Center for PTSD was created by an act of Congress in 1989 as an agency within the Veterans Administration (now the Department of Veterans Affairs) with the specific aim of helping Vietnam vets overcome the difficulties they were having in readjusting to life back in the United States. With this mandate, clinicians at Veterans Administration hospitals went to work developing a variety of methods for treating PTSD, and most of these methods are still in use today.

The clinicians and researchers who established the notion of PTSD were well aware that Vietnam was not the only potential source of traumatizing experience. As Friedman says, "The framers of the original PTSD diagnosis had in mind events such as war, torture, rape, the Nazi Holocaust, the atomic bombings of

Hiroshima and Nagasaki, natural disasters (such as earthquakes, hurricanes, and volcano eruptions) and human-made disasters (such as factory explosions, airplane crashes, and automobile accidents)."[5] In theory, then, any kind of sudden catastrophe or unexpected disaster can cause PTSD. Anything that hits a person with a violent, horrifying, life-threatening force has the potential to overwhelm his or her usual coping strategies, leaving the person vulnerable to extreme emotional distress.

In the years following PTSD's official entry into the psychiatric lexicon, the list of psychologically damaging experiences capable of producing the disorder expanded in a significant new direction. Driven by the urgings of the feminist movement to pay more attention to the long-neglected problem of domestic violence, clinicians began to recognize clear evidence of PTSD among women and children who had been victims of physical and sexual abuse. To the surprise of many in the psychiatric community, the growing body of research data on PTSD in cases of domestic abuse revealed that the disorder was affecting far more people than had initially been assumed. Taking all the potential causes of PTSD into account—the horrors of war, natural disasters, industrial accidents, and various forms of physical and sexual abuse—a national survey in 1996 estimated that a total of 5 percent of American men and 10 percent of American women have the symptoms of post-traumatic stress disorder.[6]

The official criteria for PTSD were revised in 1994 in the fourth edition of the *Diagnostic and Statistical Manual* (DSM-IV), and because they are relatively brief they may be quoted in full:

A. The person has been exposed to a traumatic event in which both of the following have been present:
   1. the person has experienced, witnessed, or been confronted with an event or events that involve actual or

threatened death or serious injury, or a threat to the physical integrity of oneself or others.

2. the person's response involved intense fear, helplessness, or horror. Note: in children, it may be expressed instead by disorganized or agitated behavior.

B. The traumatic event is persistently reexperienced in at least one of the following ways:

1. recurrent and intrusive distressing recollections of the event, including images, thoughts, or perceptions. Note: in young children, repetitive play may occur in which themes or aspects of the trauma are expressed.

2. recurrent distressing dreams of the event. Note: in children, there may be frightening dreams without recognizable content.

3. acting or feeling as if the traumatic event were recurring (includes a sense of reliving the experience, illusions, hallucinations, and dissociative flashback episodes, including those that occur upon awakening or when intoxicated). Note: in children, trauma-specific reenactment may occur.

4. intense psychological distress at exposure to internal or external cues that symbolize or resemble an aspect of the traumatic event.

5. physiologic reactivity upon exposure to internal or external cues that symbolize or resemble an aspect of the traumatic event.

C. Persistent avoidance of stimuli associated with the trauma and numbing of general responsiveness (not present before the trauma), as indicated by at least three of the following:

1. efforts to avoid thoughts, feelings, or conversations associated with the trauma.

2. efforts to avoid activities, places, or people that arouse recollections of the trauma.
3. inability to recall an important aspect of the trauma.
4. markedly diminished interest or participation in significant activities.
5. feeling of detachment or estrangement from others.
6. restricted range of affect (e.g., unable to have loving feelings).
7. sense of foreshortened future (e.g., does not expect to have a career, marriage, children, or a normal life span).

D. Persistent symptoms of increasing arousal (not present before the trauma), indicated by at least two of the following:
1. difficulty falling or staying asleep.
2. irritability or outbursts of anger.
3. difficulty concentrating.
4. hypervigilance.
5. exaggerated startle response.

E. Duration of the disturbance (symptoms in B, C, and D) is more than one month.

F. The disturbance causes clinically significant distress or impairment in social, occupational, or other important areas of functioning.[7]

It is still too early to say with any precision how many people are suffering PTSD as a direct result of the events of September 11.[8] But considering the number of wounded people, on-the-scene rescue workers, people who were uninjured but who narrowly escaped death and/or directly witnessed the destruction, and people who lost close friends, family members, and coworkers, a conservative estimate would be that several thousand people have suffered, and may continue to suffer, the symptoms of PTSD. If it is possible to acquire PTSD solely by means of watching something on television, that estimate would have to be raised by several orders of magnitude to account for the millions of people who turned on the TV on the morning of September 11 and saw the horror unfold on the screen in front of them. When these numbers are added to the national survey figures mentioned earlier, the realization begins to dawn that we are living through a time of tremendous psychological turmoil and distress.

Much remains to be learned about how people react to experiences of extreme fear, danger, and violence. For example, researchers do not have a clear understanding of why some people, when struck by sudden tragedy, develop full-blown PTSD, while other people emerge from wars, accidents, and disasters with relatively little psychological damage. It seems each person has a kind of "trauma threshold" that enables them to cope effectively with some stressful experiences but not others, and we do not yet know how exactly this threshold develops in the course of an individual's lifetime. Nor is there any clinical consensus on the most effective treatment for PTSD. Cognitive-behavioral therapy works well for some patients, but medications like Sertraline (Zoloft) work better for others. People with moderate cases of PTSD respond positively to group therapy, although, as Friedman warns, "it is important that therapeutic goals be realistic because in some cases, PTSD is a chronic and severely debilitating psychiatric disorder that is refractory to current available treatments."[9] Putting his point in plainer language, some PTSD victims never get better no matter what they or their therapists do.

As the DSM-IV diagnosis indicates, recurrent nightmares and disrupted sleep are prominent symptoms of PTSD, and much research has been conducted specifically on the question of what can be done to stop the trauma-related dreams and restore people's normal sleep patterns. Several investigators (including Rosalind Cartwright, Milton Kramer, Ernest Hartmann, Barry Krakow, and Deirdre Barrett[10]) have developed a general consensus about the nature and meaning of PTSD nightmares, and this consensus view has strongly influenced the caregiving practices of therapists, pastoral counselors, social workers, facilitators of support groups, and various other health care professionals. Hartmann gives an especially articulate description of current thinking about PTSD nightmares in his book *Dreams and Nightmares: The New Theory on the Origin and Meaning of Dreams*.[11]

According to Hartmann, the function of PTSD nightmares is to make *connections* between the traumatizing event and the rest of the dreamer's life, thus helping the person repair his or her sense of meaning, safety, and order in the world. Hartmann points to a significant pattern in the nightmares that many other clinicians working with PTSD victims have reported: the initial nightmares are extremely vivid reenactments of the traumatizing experience, but as time passes the dream content gradually becomes more symbolic, more "dreamy," with increasing references to the rest of the individual's life.[12] Clinicians now take it as a strongly positive sign of progress and healing when the dreams of a person suffering PTSD make this transition from literal replayings to symbolic imaginings.[13] For Hartmann, this pattern demonstrates the beneficial function of dreaming and its capacity to make connections more broadly and inclusively than is usually possible in waking life.[14] Although PTSD nightmares can be extremely upsetting, Hartmann says they are serving a "quasi-therapeutic" function that is essential to the healing process. Like any effective type of psychotherapy, dreaming provides people with a safe place (safe in the sense that the dreamer is asleep, temporarily immobilized, and turned away from the outer world) in which the painful feelings from the traumatizing event may, over time, be moderated and integrated into the rest of life. Hartmann says, "Gradually, guided by the sequence of emotions, the traumatic event is connected up, woven in, placed within whatever contexts are available in the dreamer's memory systems."[15]

All of this is important background information to have in mind as we try to understand the meaning of dreams and nightmares that come in response to an unexpected crisis like a terrorist attack, a hurricane, a sexual assault, a house fire, or a car accident. The approach I present in this book takes its point of departure from the findings of Hartmann and other PTSD researchers. I make frequent reference to their studies, even as I suggest that the mainstream view of PTSD nightmares is ultimately inadequate and must be revised. To put it briefly, the mainstream approach to PTSD suffers from a deficient understanding of human health and vitality. Health is not simply the absence of illness, yet psychologists have for the most part failed to provide a clear and accurate account of what constitutes non-pathological human functioning. This problem has recently been addressed by members of the "positive psychology" movement, and while I will not comment here on the substance of their proposals I do share their concern that psychologists, particularly those working in clinical and therapeutic contexts, need to expand their awareness of human strengths, virtues, and creative capacities.

This need is especially pressing with regard to dreams and nightmares. As I show in the chapters to come, the frightening dreams that emerge in response to unexpected disasters are doing much more than simply connecting a given trauma to prior memories and restoring a sense of normality to life. I argue that dreams are in fact a vital element in the struggle of trauma victims to create *new* meanings, explore *new* dimensions of reality, and envision *new* possibilities for the future. Reaching that stage in the healing process does not happen quickly or easily, and for some PTSD victims it never happens at all. But my basic goal in this book is to persuade readers that such a stage *does exist* and needs to be more fully recognized and appreciated by caregivers working with trauma victims. The process of healing from an unexpected disaster aims at something beyond "normalization," beyond the restoration of emotional mastery and self-control. The healing process ultimately aims toward a renewal of the individual's capacity for creative living. I do not believe the mainstream view of PTSD among mental health professionals is sufficiently attentive to this process, and my hope is that *Dreams of Healing* will supplement current caregiving theory and practice with a more vigorous and dynamic understanding of healthy human existence.

As an opening illustration of my approach, let me share one of the first dreams I heard following the September 11 attack. It came from a thirty-eight-year-old woman I will call "Melissa," who told me this:

Two nights after the event, I dreamed I had a new job in the WTC. It was on one of the uppermost floors. I knew what was going to happen but for some reason could not tell the other people in the office, nor could I leave the building until I knew what date it was. I remember walking up to one of the glass walls and looking down to the ground, very, very far below. There were no calendars anywhere in the offices, nor did the computers have the date/time on their desktop. I kept running from office to office asking different people, "What is the date?" Everyone ignored the question, as though I had said nothing. Instead, they kept wanting to greet me and welcome me to the company. I was frantic to know the date, but no one would tell me. At some point in this horrible loop I woke up.[16]

In response to my question about any connection she might have to the World Trade Center or the attack of September 11, Melissa said, "I have never even been to New York City. I live in a peaceful little spot of Western Montana; however, in 1992 I worked [as a nurse] for a year in an Islamic fundamentalist country: Saudi Arabia. It was the longest year of my life. That year had

9

a powerful effect on me and this disaster has brought it to the forefront of my consciousness again. Unlike most Americans who have never lived in a country like that, I know firsthand how much the extremists hate us and our way of life and the events of the past ten days [she was telling me this on September 21] terrify me beyond belief."[17]

Even with this brief description, it is clear that at one level Melissa's nightmare is making connections between the horrible events of September 11 and the comparably horrible events of her year in Saudi Arabia. As Hartmann and other researchers have found, a present tragedy frequently has the unfortunate effect of reactivating past experiences of fear, helplessness, and danger. "Trauma often 'rekindles' memories of an older trauma, and the dreams often refer to older traumatic situations involving the same emotion."[18] Seen from this perspective, Melissa's nightmare expresses her fearful realization that what happened on September 11 has many similarities to what she experienced in Saudi Arabia. Following Hartmann's thinking, Melissa's dream has a quasi-therapeutic value in the way it emotionally contextualizes the events of September 11. Perhaps the dream will remind Melissa of successful coping strategies from the past that could be of use to her in recovering from September 11—if something helped her deal with the Saudi Arabia experience ten years ago, maybe it can help her now in this new but similar emotional situation.

All of these ideas occurred to me when I first heard Melissa describe her dream, and I could see how well her experience conformed to the mainstream approach. Still, I had questions. For example, why the specific focus on the date? As a general hermeneutic strategy I feel a good starting point for the understanding of any particular dream is to focus on the most vivid element in the dream, the point of greatest energy, intensity, and vitality. Melissa's frantic effort to find out the date certainly seemed to be this dream's most vivid element. Where is this intense emotional energy coming from? I was also struck by the metaphorical possibilities of the question, "What is the date?," and I wondered if Melissa's urgent need to answer it in the dream symbolically reflected any of the existential concerns that so many people felt in the aftermath of September 11.

I asked Melissa about all this, and I asked her more broadly if she could say anything more about her experiences in Saudi Arabia, for example whether she was a target of specific hostility or was just generally aware of anti-American sentiment during her stay. This is how she replied:

> As Western women in Saudi we were constantly the focus of hostility any time we left the grounds of King Faisal Hospital. We were spit upon and one of the members of my department was standing outside a local store and felt a sharp sting on her back. She discovered a Saudi woman had run a sharp instrument across the back of her *abayah* (the long black garment we all had to wear outside the hospital) and cut it completely off. While I was there several Western nurses disappeared and were never found.
>
> One evening I was walking to an adjoining American compound, just across the street. It was dark and there was no one else out. I realized a dark van was driving slowly behind me. They passed me and slowed down; the side door of the van opened very slowly as though someone was about to jump out. I was terrified because no one else was around. I started walking faster, though that would take me in closer proximity to the van, because I saw a gate up ahead to the compound. When I reached the gate, the van door closed loudly and the van drove off quickly. All Western women had to live in apartments on the grounds of the hospital. At

night we would have to disconnect our phones because our numbers were sold to Saudi males in the city who would call all night long with obscene statements and suggestions. They would pull up beside us in their Mercedes, holding their hands out with gold chains, asking us to come with them. If we went to the local malls, the *mutaawa* or religious police, would constantly harass us, sometimes striking us on the back of the legs with camel whips and calling us "American whores." They would have no medical care in Saudi were it not for the thousands of medical support personnel from the U.S., Canada, England, Ireland, Australia, and New Zealand, yet we were daily stalked and reviled for the freedom we have in our own countries. It left a deep and lasting impression on my psyche. I have joked for the last ten years about PTSD, but the events since September 11 have stirred it all up again. I didn't need to witness what happened at the WTC and the Pentagon to know how very much Islamic fundamentalists hate us.

As for my dream, the main focus being the date was something I just interpreted literally. For some reason, in the dream I knew I could not physically leave the building until I knew the date. There was an urgency about it and no one would/could tell me the date. I knew what was going to happen but was trapped there until I could confirm what day it was. Of course, the more abstract interpretation is that we now find ourselves in an unknown/uncertain time. We feel on a gut level that something bad is about to happen but we cannot act because we don't know when it will happen. This is a dark and terrifying time and none of us knows what the final outcome will be. A "holy Jihad" may be worse than anything America has ever seen in any of its previous wars.

Melissa's comments fill out the personal life context of her nightmare and point to several different levels of meaning. She says she used to "joke" about suffering from PTSD as a result of her experiences in Saudi Arabia, but she doesn't seem to be laughing now. The September 11 terrorist attack opened all of that up again, bringing back the raw, painful feelings from that time. For a year Melissa lived in a continual state of anxiety, in a culture of extreme gender segregation, where American women were both hated and lusted after. Threatening male sexuality was pervasive, and Melissa clearly felt an ever-present sense of personal physical danger. Although she describes at length the sexual threats made against her and the other nurses, this element is not explicitly present in the dream. Still, the setting of the dream—in one of the uppermost floors of the tall WTC towers, from which she can look down to the ground very, very far below—has a phallic dimension to it, and you don't have to be a Freudian analyst to suspect that the motivation behind the terrorists' choice of the WTC towers as targets involved a kind of phallic aggressiveness, with its goal being the symbolic castration of American economic power.

In any case, what is noteworthy is that Melissa's dream does *not* make direct reference to the sexual aspect of her traumatizing experiences in Saudi Arabia. What carries over from those experiences, and what is evidently most relevant for her present situation, is a powerful sense of fear, dread, and isolation: *she knows something no one else knows*. In the dream Melissa realizes there is a dangerous, frightening disjunction between her and all the people around her. She knows the attack is coming and wants to find out the date, but no else will listen or take her seriously. This is the same way she felt in Saudi Arabia (when she was stalked by predatory males on a daily basis even though she knew she was providing their country with essential health care services), and also in the days immediately following September 11 ("Unlike most Americans who have never lived in a country like that, I know firsthand how much the extremists hate us and our way of life..."). The dream thus acts as a kind of emotional conduit, carrying significant feelings from her past into conscious awareness and clarifying important features of her present situation. The emotional intensity of the dream reflects her urgent yearning to *make sense* of the chaos around her—a fundamentally creative yearning that, while deeply shaken, has not been destroyed by the trauma and remains a vital strength in her life.

What, then, is "the meaning" of Melissa's dream? As I said in the introduction, I do not believe the meaning of any dream can be reduced to a simple phrase or formula. Every dream has multiple dimensions of significance, some of which can be identified fairly quickly and others that require more time and effort to discern. On one level, Melissa's dream brings back to conscious awareness her feelings from the time she spent in Saudi Arabia, literally "re-minding" her that she still suffers terrible emotional wounds from those experiences. On another level, her dream orients her attention toward something she knows but many other Americans do not, namely the intense hatred that Muslim extremists feel toward the United States. Perhaps her dream also expresses a hint of domestic criticism, aimed at those Americans who remain oblivious to that dire threat and who cheerfully try to welcome her into their doomed company.

On still another level, Melissa's dream marks an awareness of the tremendous historical importance of the attack. September 11, 2001, will surely be remembered as a watershed event in American history, comparable to the December 7, 1941, Japanese attack on Pearl Harbor, and the November 23, 1963, assassination of John F. Kennedy. Those events profoundly changed the nation, and most of us feel September 11 will have the same transformative impact, although we are still anxiously unclear about what exactly the long-term consequences will be. In this sense, none of us knows "what the date is"; none of us knows what September 11 is going to mean in our lives. As Melissa says, "We feel on a gut level that something bad is about to happen but we cannot act because we don't know when it will happen."

And, to mention one last level of meaning, her dream reflects the continued healthy functioning of her creative imagination, no small matter for someone who has just been struck by a massive community disaster and who is in danger of being overwhelmed by paralyzing fears and agonizing memories.

I suspect many other levels of meaning could be discerned in Melissa's nightmare. The dream may have additional significance for her family relations, her personal health, her work experiences, and several other aspects of her life. How far one goes in exploring such possibilities depends, of course, on what one is trying to learn. For our purposes I want to stop here and reflect on what has come of this relatively brief discussion of Melissa's nightmare. The material presented so far—a dream, some initial comments about it, and answers to a handful of follow-up questions—is the sort of information that I expect caregivers working in almost any context could easily gather from the people with whom they are working. In this sense (and perhaps this sense only) there is no real mystery to working with dreams. All you have to do is let people know you're interested in listening. When a sudden tragedy strikes, people almost always experience a big upsurge in vivid nightmares, but far too rarely do trauma victims find anyone who is genuinely willing to discuss their strange, unsettling dream experiences. This, I suggest, is a tremendous opportunity for caregivers: listening to dreams is the clearest, most direct, most easily accessed means of gaining insight into people's emotional suffering following an unexpected disaster.

Nan's Dream Series

As a counterpoint to the dreams of Melissa and others that came in response to the collective crisis of September 11, I want to share the dreams and nightmares of Nan, who suffered a terrible personal crisis in the form of a serious car accident. The same dreamwork methods that can be used to help the victims of huge catastrophes can also be used in caregiving with individuals who have been struck by private disasters that may be small-scale in comparison with something like September 11 but nevertheless are emotionally devastating to the people who experience them.

Nan is a fifty-seven-year-old woman from Louisiana who came to California for graduate school in the ministry. In the fall of 2001 Nan was involved in a serious car accident in which she suffered three broken vertebra in her neck. She was taken by ambulance to a hospital and had to wait five days in the Intensive Care Unit, heavily sedated on morphine, before undergoing an eight-hour-long surgery to repair the damage to her neck. After the surgery she did physical therapy to strengthen her left-side extremities, which were very weakened but not permanently damaged. She could not raise her left arm above her waist for several weeks. Fortunately, Nan was able to continue with her schooling, and she eventually recovered all her physical abilities, although six months after the accident she still felt decidedly slower and weaker than she had been before.

At the beginning of the chapter we heard Nan's first remembered dreams after the accident—an incessant stream of nightmarish imagery (it doesn't get much worse than "demons from Hell") and acute emotional distress. Here are the next three dreams Nan experienced during her hospital stay:

2. I have "forgotten" my baby, now I'm trying to find it but I have shit all over me including my glasses so I can't see. I find it, it feels cool and I thump it in my hand (kinda a smack on its bottom), but I can't see any-

thing. I don't know whether it's dead or alive. "They" come and take the baby away from me but I don't know if I'm 'guilty' of abusing it or it me! I can't see; I don't know anything. How could I have forgotten my baby! Darts are hitting me and sticking in me but I can't see to defend myself! I don't know where they are coming from!

3. I am aware that I am in a flat, a dark flat with other abandoned children.

4. Later going downstairs into a girls' bedroom. It is very attractive, decorated with a "Benetton" theme—even silver Benatton sneakers that seem to move as they play/sing a theme song. The front of the shoes opened like lips and merrily sang. Everything looks very well cared for—pampered. A very well kept room of a young woman who appears to have it all—at least she does a lot of shopping going by the open boxes and new clothes lying around. I hear water running—the shower. I walk to the bathroom and there are 2 white plastic tubs with wet clothes soaking and a young woman lying on the floor of the white tile shower with H2O running onto her and there is a feint tinge of pink (blood) swirling around her and in the water of the tubs. That is the only color in the room: that pale pink tinge and her long dark hair. She is as white as the tile; the life seems to be ebbing out of her. She barely opens her eyes and looks at me. "Can you help me," she pleads. She thinks she is going to die, but I know she is not. The/her bleeding has taken over her life. There is almost no life left in her—everything is pale.

Nan said these dreams were almost surely influenced by the anesthesia from her surgery and the highly potent pain medications she was given following surgery. The curtains in her first dream had the same damask pattern as the actual curtains surrounding her hospital bed, and she immediately associated the dark flat in her third dream with the hospital ward she lay in. Nan felt the abandoned children symbolized the five older women in the hospital ward with her, all of them there for hip replacement surgery.

17

One remarkable feature of Nan's first four dreams is what they do *not* contain: any direct, literal reference to the car accident. Like Melissa's dream of the World Trade Center, Nan's four dreams focus not on the details of the traumatizing event but rather on its emotional impact—in Nan's case, feelings of fear, helplessness, confusion, and vulnerability. These feelings come through very clearly in her dreams, even if the imagery has no immediately obvious connection to the car accident that caused them. Indeed, the imagery in Nan's first four dreams is quite bizarre—demons from Hell, a strange baby, abandoned children, a nearly lifeless young woman. It would be hard to say anything definitive about Nan's situation (beyond the sheer intensity of her emotional distress) based on the wild, seemingly random imagery of these dreams. Of course, many tantalizing possibilities appear when we read through Nan's dreams, and many interesting questions arise. What is it about the damask curtains in dream number 1 that generates such terror? What does the baby in the second dream symbolize—new life? Vulnerability? Dependence on the care of others? What has happened to the young woman in dream 4? If Nan knows that the young woman won't die, does that mean Nan also knows somewhere inside her that she herself won't die?

I imagine readers will have come up with several questions of their own, questions that can't be answered without having more information about Nan and her situation. In later chapters we discuss several other dreams Nan experienced, and my hope is that readers will see how the seemingly random elements in Nan's first four dreams turn out to be the opening expression of themes in her later dreams that directly relate to her healing process. The remarkable progression of Nan's dreams over the six months following her accident illustrates the value of analyzing not just individual dreams, but whole series of dreams. C. G. Jung was the first modern psychologist to make this point, and this is how he put it:

"Every interpretation is an hypothesis, an attempt to read an unknown text. An obscure dream, taken in isolation, can hardly ever be interpreted with any certainty. For this reason I attach little importance to the interpretation of single dreams. A relative degree of certainty is reached only in the interpretation of a series of dreams, where the later dreams correct the mistakes we have made in handling those that went before. Also, the basic ideas and themes can be recognized much better in a dream-series."[19]

Following the development of images, themes, and symbols across a series of dreams is without question the most reliable way of interpreting any single dream. Images that made no sense when examined in isolation can take on surprising new significance when considered in connection with dreams that came before and after. Of course, having a dream series is no guarantee of hermeneutic accuracy. Even if you have a long series of dreams before you, there will likely be several elements that can never be satisfactorily explained or accounted for.

The Therapeutic Value of Dreamsharing

Given current psychiatric knowledge about PTSD, you might assume that hospital workers would expect a high incidence of nightmares among their patients and would be trained to respond accordingly. Sadly, that does not seem to be the case. Several months after Nan's accident, when she had time to reflect on her horrifying experiences in the hospital, she said, "Although I had-have complete confidence in the medical professionals involved in my care, they didn't want to hear about nightmares, etc. They offered me pain medications to help me sleep, but didn't mention the common occurrence of nightmares after trauma or surgery. We certainly didn't discuss what might be happening, or its possible healing benefits."[20] If Nan's experience is at all representative of what happens (or doesn't happen) in other hospitals, patients are being done an incredible disservice, and hospital workers are neglecting a powerful resource and valuable ally in their caregiving work.

The good news is that the basic principles of dreamsharing are easy to learn and apply to almost any form of caregiving, in hospitals or in other settings. I want to underscore the accessibility of dream-generated insights because sometimes people think dream interpretation requires special techniques that only professional psychiatrists with extensive training are qualified to use. The increasing professionalization of psychotherapy in recent years has created the illusion of a vast gap between the specialized knowledge of psychological experts and the unschooled "folk beliefs" of everyone else. The fact is, humans were sharing, discussing, and learning from their dreams for many, many years before professional psychotherapists came on the scene. Every known culture throughout history has developed detailed beliefs about the nature of dreams and methods to interpret their meanings.[21] Although specialized training can be helpful in trying to understand dreams, it is by no means necessary. The basic principles of dream interpretation can be successfully applied by anyone who takes the time to listen carefully, ask good, open-ended questions, and respect the dreamer's own emerging insights about the given dream. I feel very strongly that sharing dreams is a natural, normal part of human life, and I lament the trend in Western mental health care over the past century to confine dream interpretation within a strictly psychotherapeutic context.

Let me be clear that I am *not* minimizing the value or importance of specialized treatment for acute cases of PTSD. Trauma victims who are so badly damaged they can no longer take care of their own basic physical needs should receive immediate attention from health care professionals with training in PTSD treatment, and I encourage caregivers to become familiar with the professional health care services available in their areas for help in such situations. Having said that, let me also be clear that many people who experience a sudden tragedy do *not* develop full-blown PTSD. They are able to continue with the activities of their lives, although they suffer deep emotional wounds that generate many of the symptoms of PTSD. For these people (perhaps the majority of those affected by a communal disaster like September 11), specialized treatment is not absolutely necessary, and the caregiving efforts of "non-specialist" counselors, clergy, teachers, friends, and family members can be wonderfully effective in helping them mourn their losses and create new meaning in their lives.

The point I am leading to is that in a time of sudden crisis and tragedy, when people are suffering terribly in both their waking and dreaming lives, caregivers should have no hesitation in actively inviting people to talk about their nightmares. If skilled and experienced psychotherapists are available to help in this process, so much the better; but no one in a caregiving capacity should doubt his or her own ability to work effectively with dream material as a means of helping people in pain.

Think back to Melissa's nightmare, and what we learned in our brief study of it. In the course of describing her dream, Melissa was able to express a complex array of emotions, highlight the vital relevance of her past experiences for her current crisis, reflect on the possible future implications for herself and her community, and demonstrate the enduring vitality of her creative imagination. All of this valuable information about her emotional situation came simply by means of talking for a few moments about a dream. Although in the chapters to come I offer several different questions, techniques, and strategies that can further enhance the practice of dream interpretation, the fundamental process requires nothing more than this: a willingness to listen, a respect for the dreamer, and an openness to new meanings.

Essential Bibliography

Barrett, Deirdre, ed. 1996. *Trauma and Dreams*. Cambridge: Harvard University Press.

Bulkeley, Kelly, ed. 2001a. *Dreams: A Reader on the Religious, Cultural, and Psychological Dimensions of Dreaming*. New York: Palgrave.

Cartwright, Rosalind. 1991. Dreams That Work: The Relation of Dream Incorporation to Adaptation of Stressful Events. *Dreaming* 1 (1):3–10.

Friedman, Matthew J. 2002. *Post-Traumatic Stress Disorder: An Overview*. National Center for PTSD.

Galea, Sandor, Jennifer Ahern, Heidi Resnick, Dean Kilpatrick, Michael Bucuvalas, Joel Gold, & David Vlahov. 2002. Psychological Sequelae of the September 11 Terrorist Attacks in New York City. *New England Journal of Medicine* 346 (13):982–87.

Hartmann, Ernest. 1984. *The Nightmare: The Psychology and Biology of Terrifying Dreams*. New York: Basic Books.

———. 1995. Making Connections in a Safe Place: Is Dreaming Psychotherapy? *Dreaming* 5 (4):213–28.

———. 1998. *Dreams and Nightmares: The New Theory on the Origin and Meaning of Dreams*. New York: Plenum.

Jung, C. G. 1975. The Practical Use of Dream Analysis. In *Dreams*. Original ed., 1934. Princeton: Princeton University Press.

Krakow, Barry, D. Tandberg, M. Barey, & L. Scriggins. 1995. Nightmares and Sleep Disturbance in Sexually Assaulted Women. *Dreaming* 5 (3):199–206.

Kramer, Milton. 1991. The Nightmare: A Failure in Dream Function. *Dreaming* 1 (4):277–86.

Night Terrors: Trauma Can Spark Nightmares—and Also Aid Healing. 2001. *New York Newsday*, 10/10.

Ochberg, Frank M. 1991. Gift from Within: Posttraumatic Therapy. *Psychotherapy* 28 (1):1–20.

Sternberg, Esther M. 2002. Brain-Immune Connections in Health and Disease. Paper read at Science and Mind/Body Medicine, May 2, Boston, Massachusetts.

Notes

1. Night Terrors 2001.
2. Personal communication, 6/1/02. Here as in all other quoted dreams from the Nan series, I have reproduced the spelling and grammar exactly as she wrote them in her journal.
3. Friedman 2002, 1–2.
4. Sternberg 2002.
5. Friedman 2002, 1.
6. Friedman 2002, 3.
7. DSM-IV 309.81. According to Frank Ochberg, a psychiatrist at Michigan State University, reading aloud with a client the DSM criteria for PTSD can be a clinically useful experience: I will never forget the first time I brought out my green, hard-bound copy of the DSM-III, moved my chair next to Mrs. M., and showed her the chapter on PTSD. Mrs. M. is a thin, soft-spoken woman in her thirties who was assaulted and raped in South Lansing, Michigan. She was referred by a colleague and had just finished telling me her symptoms, 8 or 9 weeks after the traumatic event. She was frightened, guarded, perplexed, and sad. She had no basis for trusting me. But after she saw the words in the book, as I read them aloud, she brightened, sat up tall, and said, "You mean, that's me, in that book! I never thought this could be real!" Seldom have I found such a reversal of mood and such a sudden establishment of trust and rapport since Mrs. M., but I have never missed an opportunity to read the criteria list with a client, when it seemed appropriate. (Ochberg 1991, 4)
8. A study published in the *New England Journal of Medicine* (Galea et al. 2002) estimated that the prevalence of acute

PTSD among Manhattan residents was 7.5 percent the period five to nine weeks after September 11, and the prevalence of depression was 9.7 percent. Both figures are approximately twice the average for acute PTSD and depression in the general population. Among residents who lived south of Canal Street (close to the World Trade Center), the prevalence of PTSD was 20 percent.

9. Friedman 2002, 7.
10. Cartwright 1991; Hartmann 1998, 1995, 1984; Krakow et al. 1995; Kramer 1991; Barrett 1996.
11. Hartmann 1998.
12. Barrett 1996, 3.
13. Perhaps the same process was involved in the decisions of the *New York Times* to create a separate section of the newspaper ("A Nation Challenged") for all September 11-related stories, and then fold that section back into the regular paper once the immediate intensity of the disaster had receded to manageable proportions.
14. Hartmann 1998, 3.
15. Hartmann 1998, 25.
16. Personal communication, 9/21/01.
17. Personal communication, 9/21/01.
18. Hartmann 1998, 27.
19. Jung 1975, 98.
20. Personal communication, 5/27/02.
21. Bulkeley 2001a.

2. Ripple Effects

Ground Zero Dreaming

In any kind of communal disaster, people's emotional reactions involve a mix of personal and collective concerns. A shocking blow to the community at large echoes and reverberates painfully within the psyche of many individuals. Massive social tragedies like September 11 can trigger a painful resurgence of private conflicts and anxieties that, in many cases, people have been vainly struggling for years to overcome. This is why the psychological damage from communal disasters usually extends far beyond those who suffer direct physical or economic harm, wreaking havoc in the lives of people who are already existing at the edge of their coping abilities.

Evidence for this psychological "ripple" effect came to me from Roger Knudson, a psychotherapist and Director of Clinical Training in the Psychology Department at Miami University of Ohio. Roger is a friend and dream research colleague, and I contacted him late in the fall of 2001 to ask his impression of the clinical consequences of September 11. He replied,

> The overall demand for therapy in this area this fall went off the charts. In our private practice group, managed care had for several years caused considerable constriction of referrals—though by the end of 2000 that had already turned around. But from 9/11 on, the phone never stopped ringing. We ended up with a waiting list for the first time in probably seven or eight

years because we ran out of places to refer new cases—suggesting to me that all of the therapists in the area were also swamped. The Psychology Clinic at the university had more crisis walk-in cases than we had ever had, with records going back to the mid-70s. The University Student Counseling Center was swamped and on a waiting list by early October—weeks earlier than is typical for them in the fall.

My impression is that whatever problems people had before the attack were suddenly brought to the surface. The foundations for everyone suddenly wobbled and old defensive patterns were suddenly less effective. So people who had been avoiding therapy or managing without it suddenly decided it was time for professional help.[1]

Roger said he himself had heard surprisingly few dreams with explicit imagery from September 11, "so I think you might want to note that those people who did dream directly about the attacks may be viewed against the more general background of the many individuals whose psychological balance was seriously upset by the attacks and subsequent upheaval in the national consciousness."[2] Roger's point is well taken. The emotional distress that gets stirred up by a collective crisis does not always express itself in terms that explicitly connect to the crisis. This has important practical implications for caregivers, because it means that a disaster in the broader community can cause deep psychological suffering for people *even if the people themselves are not aware of the disaster as a source of their suffering*. Caregivers thus need to apply an element of sociological analysis in their work if they want to understand fully the emotional troubles of people who seem far removed from a collective tragedy but who nevertheless have been deeply impacted by it.

In addition to Roger, I asked several other friends and colleagues whose work involves listening to people's dreams about their experiences since September 11, and they reported several interesting changes in dream content, emotionality, and frequency. For example, Charles McPhee, who hosts a syndicated radio talk show and an interactive Web site devoted to dreams, told me,

> Yes, I have noticed a definite increase in the number of bomb dreams and separation from family dreams. Also end-of-the-world dreams, in that a mother of some young children keeps dreaming that she is in a cave with her husband that is collapsing from which she can't escape (bin Laden), followed by being in a shopping mall that blows up (terrorist attack), followed by watching a neighboring city burn to the ground (terrorist attack, war). Dreams that reflect uncertainty about the future, and fear of terrorist attacks striking near home. In New York the war theme appears to enter more literally. Mothers loading up AK 47s for other troops and soldiers, riding in the back of open trucks and jeeps with large guns attached to them. Family members who are separated from each other dream of inability to reach the family member on the cell phone, or that the distant family member has died. When terror strikes, we all want to be close to our family.[3]

Kathleen Sullivan, host of the *Dreams: Another Way of Knowing* radio program on KAZU public radio in the Monterey Bay region of California, says the main difference she has noticed is a rise in the appearance of Middle Eastern people as "bad guys." And it's not just the men who are threatening, as Kathleen notes, "I have heard three dreams in which Middle Eastern women and children were also considered threatening or to be avoided."[4]

Karen Bellitto, a clinical social worker in a palliative care hospital in New York, told me she had heard several dreams in which people envisioned themselves on the top floors of the World Trade Center towers, watching the planes flying at them, crashing into the building, and exploding in flames. She said what made the dreams so terrifying was the people's felt experience of *knowing* they were going to die—it wasn't a quick death, but one that gave them a few agonizing moments to face, in full conscious awareness, the end of their lives.[5]

Reports like these are suggestive of a remarkably broad-ranging influence of September 11 on people's dreams, although I would add that caution should be used in making claims any stronger than that. It is extremely difficult to conduct systematic empirical research on a phenomenon as vast as the changing dream patterns of a nation, and right now no one can say for sure if their observations represent more general trends in the population at large or simply reflect the particularities of their own experiences. This is why I say the comments are *suggestive*—they point to intriguing possibilities in the experiences of other people, but they are not absolutely definitive of what *must* be happening to all people in all parts of the country. Here as elsewhere, dream interpretation requires what Aristotle called *phronesis* or practical wisdom, the ability to discern the truth in a particular concrete situation.[6] Interpreting dreams ultimately demands a capacity to understand the uniqueness, the immediate specificity, the sheer "thisness" of each individual dream. Keeping that point firmly in mind, I suggest you regard the observations of people like Roger, Charles, Kathleen, and Karen (and me as well!) not as authoritative declarations of all-embracing truth but rather as potentially thought-provoking enrichments of your efforts to understand the dreams of yourself and others.

In that spirit, I would like to discuss a dream with some striking symbolic patterns that I believe reflect similar patterns in the dreams of many other people who were physically distant from the site of the September 11 attack but who felt a vivid and immediate emotional connection to Ground Zero.

The dream was told to me by a forty-two-year-old woman named Julie, a single mother living in Indiana who had no personal connection to the September 11 attack. It is an unusually long dream, with the first several scenes involving family members and friends in the stands at a baseball game talking with each other, walking around, and eating and drinking. Then the setting of the dream shifts:

A couple of friends and I left the baseball game and went to another place. I don't know what the place was. It was a semi-circle theater. The round stage was completely dark except for a spotlight on the man speaking. The back half of the round stage had individual dark curtains. Each curtain had the name of a place in lights. One of them was Sanders Lake (the name of an amusement park my parents used to take us when we were children). We chose that curtain.

Immediately we were transported to another place. I thought it was going to be Sanders Lake but it wasn't. This is difficult to describe. It looked as though we were watching a movie scanning the night skyline of a large city, but at the same time it felt as though we were there—not physically flying and not in an airplane—which is why it is difficult to describe that part. But now it is suddenly daytime and we fly past the World Trade Center towers and they are on fire and smoking. I realize where we are and when and I become very upset and fight back tears.

The significance of the WTC towers in Julie's dream derives in the first place from its specific location in the dreaming narrative. In the opening scenes of the dream Julie is with her friends and family at a baseball game, but then somehow she finds herself in a strange theater setting, confronted by a row of mysterious dark curtains. The atmosphere is like an eerie game show or a minimalist play; there's dramatic tension in the uncertainty of what lies behind the curtains. Above one of the curtains Julie sees in lights the name of an amusement park, a family vacation spot from her childhood. She and her friends choose that curtain—and suddenly the scene shifts, to a city skyline at night. Suddenly the dream shifts again, now to a daytime image of the WTC towers "on fire and smoking." The harrowing September 11 image thus appears in the dream's narrative as a kind of surprise answer to the implied game show question, an unexpected climax to the strange theatrical drama.

It is helpful to focus special attention on these kinds of sudden shifts and transformations in dreams because in most cases they are points at which the dreaming imagination is bringing something *new* into the dream. A moment of sudden change in a dream is a moment when novel possibilities and insights are coming into the dreamer's awareness, when new connections are being made across different realms of life, when the dreamer is confronting aspects of reality that he or she may never have consciously noticed or thought about before. In Julie's case she chooses a curtain that harkens back to happy childhood memories, then experiences two abrupt shifts in the dream's setting, a double decentering of her perspective. First she is given a movie-like view of a city's night skyline and, momentarily, she becomes personally part of the city ("At the same time it felt as though we were there").[7] Then she is given an aerial view of the WTC towers at the very height of that day's horrors, after the planes have hit and just before the collapse ("I realize where we are and when"), and this realization evokes a strong and sorrowful emotional response in her.

Why do the WTC towers appear at this precise moment in the dream narrative, as the surprising, doubly unexpected result of Julie's choice of the "Sanders Lake" curtain? One way to answer this question is to view the WTC towers in Julie's dream as a "personal symbol," a term I developed in the course of research on political imagery in dreams.[8] When people have dreams involving a political figure like the U.S. president as a character, in many cases the image of the politician is serving as a symbolic expression of something emotionally significant in the dreamer's personal life (for example, a "presidential" part of him- or herself). The politician in the dream may reflect character qualities of leadership, authority, and "executive power," or, more critically, qualities of duplicity, insincerity, and corruption. Either way, the dream is taking a prominent cultural image from the waking world and using it as a symbolic medium by which the dreamer's own private hopes, fears, and desires may be given voice. I suggest the same thing is happening in Julie's dream, with the agonizing sight of the WTC towers burning and about to collapse symbolically expressing the many painful concerns that are currently plaguing her personal life.

Just two months earlier (she had this dream at the end of October 2001), Julie's only child, the son whom she had raised by herself and who had been her primary companion since the divorce fifteen years earlier, had left home for college. Julie had been without full-time work for almost a year, and the effort to juggle several part-time jobs while actively seeking new employment was exhausting her. In an effort to improve her credentials she was enrolled in a master's degree program at a local college, but the homework had become so burdensome she wasn't sure if she was going to have the energy to complete the program. Julie had been diagnosed with Attention Deficit Disorder several years earlier, and she used various medications to fight off the symptoms, but the most effective medication was not covered by her insurance policy, and the drug was far too expensive for her to purchase by herself. A deeply religious person, Julie prayed frequently and tried her best to maintain her faith in God despite all these difficulties. But in all honesty she couldn't help admitting, "I feel as though I am being sucked into a black hole and don't know how to get out."[9]

Her dream brings all these anxious feelings together in the image of the burning WTC towers, which at one level can be understood as a symbolic expression of her own personal life right at this moment—like the towers, Julie feels badly damaged, under attack, on the verge of collapsing. She wishes she could magically return to the comparative tranquility and happiness of childhood amusements ("Sanders Lake" beckoning in the lights above the curtain), but her dream has other ideas; it unexpectedly takes her to a place where she is compelled to witness the awful magnitude of her suffering, and to understand how her suffering fits into the context of a wider community suddenly overwhelmed with similarly intense feelings of pain, confusion, and fear.

This might sound like a pointless, if not downright cruel, thing for her dreaming imagination to do. Isn't Julie already perfectly aware of all the stressful, anxiety-provoking problems in her life? What is the dream saying that she doesn't already know? What possible value or benefit could there be to such a depressing dream?

In this regard I agree with Unitarian Universalist minister Jeremy Taylor that every dream, even the worst nightmare, has the potential to promote health and wholeness.[10] If you can dream about a problem, at some level you have strength and resources to face it—not necessarily solve it right this minute, but at least face it honestly and forthrightly, and engage actively in efforts to deal with it. When people come up against major life problems that seem to have no solution, their dreaming minds jump into overdrive and work energetically at the task of providing alternatives and possibilities not considered by waking consciousness.

I believe Julie's dream is making at least three distinct contributions to her health and wholeness: (1) It vividly dissuades her from seeking the easy escapism of nostalgia for the lost joys of the past (Sanders Lake). The narrative structure of the dream tempts her with the allure of that escapism, but then abruptly dashes her wishful expectations and forces her to focus all her emotional energy on the realities of her present situation. (2) The dream symbolically relates her personal life crisis to the collective crisis of September 11, offering her a valuable sense of solidarity with all the other people who have suffered terrible losses and are anxiously uncertain about the future. And (3) the dream guides Julie in creative new directions for possible healing and growth in the future. This emerges in the final part of her dream, when she returns to the theater, finds all her family sitting in seats, and speaks with them about their experiences with the curtains:

I was writing feverishly to get everything down on a notepad. Some people came up behind us and set up a table and sat down there. They seemed to be upper-class people. My paper was making noise as I turned the pages and they were getting very annoyed. I was having trouble finding a clean sheet of paper but did not want to stop for fear of losing some of this. Mark [Julie's son] came up to me. He is a much younger boy in this dream, maybe nine or ten. I was trying to gather all my things to go and sit with him. I had lots of papers, a drink, and a winter coat. I was having trouble getting it all. Mark helped.

Here is a second moment of intense emotion in the dream: after her strong reaction to the sight of the burning WTC towers, Julie feels a "feverish" desire to write down everything she's hearing. Writing is indeed one of Julie's greatest waking life strengths. Her most successful job experiences have always involved writing, and the one bright spot in her otherwise burdensome M.A. program is the anticipation of writing a thesis on a topic of her own choice. The pattern here is one I have seen in many dreams: In addition to revealing our worst problems with brutal, unsparing honesty, the dreams also grant us glimpses of our deepest strengths, offering grounds for genuine hope amid the many difficulties and

33

sorrows of our lives. Writing is a true source of power and creativity for Julie, and even though she feels as badly damaged as the WTC towers she still has this creative capacity within her. The dream doesn't pretend that writing is easy for her; she struggles with various obstacles (time pressure, the disapproval of "upper-class people," a lack of clean paper), but then her son Mark appears and helps her out. Even though in waking life he has grown up and left home, Mark remains a vital presence in her life, emotionally supporting her (as he did when he was nine or ten) in her continuing struggles to "gather all my things" and carry on with life.

As with Melissa's dream in chapter 1, Julie's dream undoubtedly contains several other dimensions of meaning beyond those discussed here. Julie has kept a dream journal for several years, and I am sure that if we looked carefully at her recent dream in the context of her previous ones, we would discover many new ways of understanding the dream's relevance to her personal life.[11] Someone who was working with Julie in a caregiving capacity would want to explore these possibilities in more detail, and would most likely want to focus on any recurrent characters, images, or settings that appear in this dream. For example, it would be interesting to know whether Julie has had other dreams with baseball game settings, or references to Sanders Lake, or distressing visions of urban destruction. Recurrent elements in dreams can reveal the most deeply rooted conflicts in people's lives, as well as the enduring strengths of their personalities.[12] For caregivers seeking to help relieve people's suffering, great practical insights can be gained by taking a few moments to talk about their dream lives and ask whether any current dreams seem related to other dreams they remember from the past.

For the more limited purposes of this chapter, we shall leave Julie's dream with one final observation. The vivid, unforgettable images of the WTC towers, which virtually every person in the country saw repeatedly on TV in the hours and days following September 11, have burned themselves deeply into the national psyche. The towers have become a powerful collective symbol for all the fear, confusion, and panic people felt that day. As Julie's dream indicates, the towers have also become a powerful personal symbol expressing comparably intense anxieties in people far removed from the physical site of the attack. I wonder how many other people in the country live as Julie does, with a chronic sense of impending emotional collapse? For such people, a collective disaster like September 11 only brings out into the open the painful feelings they've been suffering inside for years.

I would like to turn now to a different kind of "Ground Zero dreaming," and consider the impact of the terrorist attack on its most publicly visible victims, the rescue workers. In any kind of disaster, a number of different forces—police, firefighters, para- medics, soldiers—are called to respond immediately, and by the very nature of their jobs these professionals are regularly con- fronted with horrible suffering, destruction, and death. Of course, they themselves are subject to constant physical danger, and they must maintain a perpetually heightened state of alertness. No matter how many safety measures they take, they and their col- leagues perform their duties in an atmosphere of severe risk and danger. For all these reasons, rescue workers face particularly acute emotional challenges in the daily course of their work. If they are to manage these challenges and succeed at their jobs, they must develop a variety of psychological defenses to preserve their ability to function in crisis situations that would paralyze most people with fear and horror.

What happens, then, if a catastrophe strikes that is so mas- sive, so unexpected, and so horrific that it completely overwhelms the coping abilities even of those people who are professionally trained to deal in disaster and death? What happens if the rescue workers need rescuing?

A few days after September 11, I contacted Gloria Sturzenacker, a friend whom I have known for the past several years through the Association for the Study of Dreams (ASD). Gloria and I both have an interest in long-term dream journaling, and I first met her at a conference panel session where she presented her work on a visual symbol system to enhance the interpretive potentials of keeping a dream journal.[13] I knew that Gloria had been editor of the New York Fire Department's training magazine, and I feared that she must have known dozens of the firefighters who were killed when the WTC towers collapsed. Sadly, that was indeed the case, though because she had left the job several years earlier, she knew few of them well, and within the week she learned that her closest friends still on the job had survived. She e-mailed me back on September 18: "As a friend of mine said, there were three people he needed to know were OK, and when he found out they are, he could handle anything (such as recovering the bodies of two people from his unit, as he did on Saturday [September 15]). My three people are OK, so I'm doing better now than I was last week." She went on to say that she was trying to contribute to the emotional support efforts of the department, a process that was just beginning to be mobilized. Gloria was enough of an "insider" to know and appreciate the grueling realities of firefighting work, and yet enough of an "outsider," as a civilian and a woman, that she might provide them with a bit of safe space in which they could talk about emotions and experiences they didn't feel comfortable sharing with the other (predominantly male) firefighters.

During the next three months, Gloria attended memorial services nearly every day and spent several hours at the department headquarters helping to make calls for obituary information. She was hesitant to ask the firefighters directly about their dreams (a friend on the job had told her several years earlier, "You've got to stop talking to firefighters about dreams!"), but she did speak

36

with some who admitted they were sleeping poorly and having bad dreams. When the ASD activated the Nightmare Hotline to offer information and support for people suffering from nightmares, Gloria began handing out small batches of Hotline flyers to pass on to their coworkers. She reported that firefighters were receptive to the information in a way that would have been unimaginable before September 11. Some found that simply talking with Gloria about the hotline gave them a discreet means of expressing some of their own distressing dream experiences. She described a conversation she had with a friend in the department who considered his own reaction to be relatively unemotional: "He called today, and he was exhausted. When I told him about the Hotline, he said when he tries to go to sleep, he'll just be drifting off when he'll have a nightmare. This happens 4–5 times in a row, a different nightmare each time. Someone else told me, 'My wife nudges me during the night: "You're screaming again." "Sorry, hon.""""[14]

At yet another memorial service in December, Gloria spoke with several firefighters who voiced their concern that the *real* psychological problems were going to start after the bodies were all recovered and the funerals finished. A few days earlier, the widow of a man who worked in the WTC had committed suicide, and everyone worried that this was a harbinger of future tragedies in the department. Adding to the firefighters' distress was the highly publicized brawl that broke out at Ground Zero between firefighters and police officers, an event that led to intense media scrutiny of conflicts within the world of New York rescue workers. One person told Gloria how angry, frustrated, and isolated he and many others in the department felt about everything that had been happening to them. He asked her to help get a message out:

> He feels they [the firefighters] have been made out to
> look like thugs over the shoving incident, which he says

was actually very minor (he was there). He wants people to know firefighters are just regular people ("maybe a little less"), and they just want to be left alone to do their job. He also said firefighters are getting more and more removed from the outside world. They appreciate the fact that the public wants to do so much for them, but they feel like Vietnam vets probably felt, that no one can understand what they've been through. He thinks the idea of being told to enjoy Christmas is absurd right now. After I gave him some Nightmare Hotline flyers, we talked a bit about dreams. He said (surprise surprise!) firefighters don't like to talk about feelings. I told him one of the good things about dreams is they're like telling a story. I also mentioned some of the practical guidance and synchronicity I've gotten from my dreams. He got a bit metaphysical and spiritual about that, then said, "I didn't mean to get so deep!" and soon made an exit.[15]

The comments of Gloria's friend can help us better understand the difficult lives of rescue workers in the aftermath of a sudden, overwhelming disaster. The community's tendency to idealize rescue workers—praising them as heroes, showering them with affection, honoring them in grand public ceremonies—can have the paradoxical effect of intensifying the psychological distress of the rescue workers themselves, who may be feeling all too human in their deeply private suffering. Gloria's friend likens the firefighters to Vietnam veterans, which might seem a strange comparison given the very different public receptions of the two groups (the firefighters hailed as national heroes, the veterans shunned as painful reminders of a controversial war). But the point he makes is an important one: People who are directly involved in experiences of incredible violence and destruction (like September 11, like the Vietnam War) are scarred in ways most people will never understand. Although the public idealization may be well intentioned, it too often fails to acknowledge the actual emotional condition of the rescue workers. When Gloria's friend says that firefighters are just normal people, or "a little bit less," he gives voice to the painful disjunction some firefighters perceive between how they see themselves and how the rest of society views them. People who are suffering in this way cannot help but feel conflicted by all the exaggerated praise, cheerful reassurances, and blithe well-wishings ("Have a merry Christmas!"), which only have the effect of worsening their sense of isolation.

The analogy between the New York firefighters and Vietnam veterans can be extended in another direction that is relevant to caregiving practice. In both cases the people involved were almost exclusively male, and they were trained in a professional ethos that above all else prizes strict emotional self-control. The firefighters and veterans were taught that admitting weakness is to be avoided at all cost, because unfailing strength is the very definition of their jobs. If you need help, if you can't pull your weight, if you aren't able to keep your feelings in total control, then you shouldn't be a firefighter or a soldier.[16] Anyone who has been trained in this masculine code of "rugged individualism" (and that includes not only firefighters and soldiers but most other rescue workers as well) has been actively discouraged from ever admitting, to himself or others, the true depth of his suffering when he is struck by an overwhelming disaster.

William Genet, who runs a counseling service for police officers, a profession whose culture emphasizes "macho" values every bit as much as firefighters and soldiers, speaks of post-traumatic distress as "the invisible bullet—it goes in and nobody knows they're hit. It eats up your emotional system, your psyche."[17] Actually, I suspect that many rescue workers *do* know they have been deeply wounded, and they are yearning for some way to express their feelings and work through their pain. In the context of such an urgent need, talking about dreams can lead even skeptical people into a consideration of deeper issues. When Gloria told her firefighter friend about how meaningful her dreams had been for her, he briefly opened up and showed some real enthusiasm for emotional self-reflection ("He got a bit metaphysical and spiritual about that"). But then he became uncomfortable, made the dismissive comment "I didn't mean to get so deep!" and soon thereafter walked away. Rescue workers toughened by their experiences and their work culture may struggle to find the right language to communicate their suffering; they worry about revealing too much of their personal lives, and they fear the shameful possibility of appearing weak in front of their peers. Opening up is likely to be a lurching, on-again off-again affair.

Anyone who works in a caregiving capacity with firefighters, police officers, soldiers, and any other kind of rescue worker can expect to have experiences similar to Gloria's. Initial offerings of help and support are likely to be rebuffed, although some interest may be shown in volunteering to provide caregiving services to other coworkers. The best opportunities for caregivers to facilitate genuine emotional expression will probably come by means of indirect efforts, in special conditions of privacy and respectful sympathy.

Natural Disasters

Although nearly every American felt personally threatened by the September 11 attack and its aftermath, the fact remains that most of us face much greater chances of injury or death from natural disasters than from future terrorist attacks. Hurricanes, floods, tornadoes, blizzards, mudslides, earthquakes, volcanic eruptions, wildfires—these are the catastrophes that have plagued humankind throughout recorded history, and they continue to plague us today despite our advanced scientific knowledge and technological prowess. People who survive natural disasters usually suffer the same agonizing emotional damage as do survivors of "human-made" traumas like terrorist attacks and car accidents. Recurrent, extremely distressing nightmares are a predictable consequence of any kind of natural disaster, and caregivers who are called to help the survivors of these tragedies should be ready for a surge of bad dreams and should treat them as valuable allies in the effort to heal the survivors' physical and emotional wounds.

The best psychological study of dreams and nightmares following a natural disaster was performed by Alan Siegel, a psychotherapist in the San Francisco Bay Area, who investigated the dream patterns of people who survived the East Bay Firestorm of October 20, 1991. What began as a small, late-summer brush fire was whipped up by hot Santa Ana winds and fueled by parched grass and trees to the point where it suddenly exploded into a raging, 2,000-degree wall of flame that swept with shocking speed into the hillside neighborhoods of Oakland and Berkeley. The people living in these areas had only a few moments' warning to escape before the extremely fast-moving fire consumed their homes. Twenty-five people died, scores were burned severely, and more than 10,000 people were evacuated. A total of 3,000 homes were destroyed, rendering 5,000 people homeless.

Siegel, a resident of Berkeley who had a private psychotherapeutic practice there, moved quickly in the aftermath of the firestorm to provide nightmare help for survivors. He worked closely with forty-two people, twenty-eight who lost their homes (Fire Survivors) and fourteen who lived in the burn zone but whose homes were not destroyed (Fire Evacuees). Siegel's most surprising finding was that the Fire Evacuees had worse nightmares than the Fire Survivors: "Their [the Fire Evacuees'] unremitting survivor guilt, depression, intrusive thought, and nightmares were more distressing than that of the Fire Survivors. In addition, the Evacuees' dreams were more focused on death, bodily injury, and disaster and had more manifest content references to the events of the Firestorm than those of the Survivors, who actually lost property."[18] Siegel says the Survivors were fortunate to have external activities to focus their attention on (finding a new home, dealing with insurance companies), while the Evacuees "had no map of activities…to chart their recovery and distract them from their inner preoccupations."[19] The Survivors received extensive sympathy and support from the community, while the Evacuees were widely thought to be the "lucky ones" who had escaped real harm. Privately, though, many of the Evacuees struggled with intense feelings of guilt about their apparent good fortune, and like the Survivors they were acutely sensitive to the possibility of new dangers in the world. An example of an Evacuee's dream comes from a woman named Andrea, who returned to the burn zone the next day to find that her home was the only structure left standing in her neighborhood:

What I recall is an absolutely terrifying nightmare in which the fire had developed an organic consciousness. It was the embodiment of evil. It hid itself very well up on the hill in a pile of brush where it waited for all the fire departments to leave. Then it came back to get the houses it had missed. Somehow it had marked these houses with a fire seed and all it had to do was pass by the fire seeds for the house to ignite. I woke up screaming because I saw our "fire seed" begin to swell. In the dream, I was alone in the house.[20]

Siegel suggests that people like Andrea may *appear* to be fine and in no need of special help, but in fact they are suffering from deep emotional wounds that are all the more painful because they seem so insignificant in comparison to what other people are experiencing. "Results of our study suggest that special attention be given to the hidden wounds of the 'lucky' survivors of a trauma."[21] This is good caregiving advice, and Siegel's work supports the point we have already considered, that the painful emotional ripples of a collective disaster (whether natural or human-induced) spread far beyond those who lose property or are physically injured. Another important point from Siegel's study is this: "Our results suggest that people who have 'near-miss' encounters with trauma may be especially vulnerable if they have a history of multiple or severe loss, trauma, or deprivation."[22] Translated into a practical maxim, this means that caregivers should, whenever they encounter a person who was not directly affected by a disaster but who is suffering strong PTSD symptoms, explore the possibility that the disaster has reactivated the person's conflicted, unresolved feelings about a trauma from the past.

As a psychotherapist, Siegel was not focusing on spiritual issues in his study. But Andrea's mention of the fire seed as the "embodiment of evil" raises an issue that is probably familiar to caregivers who work in religious or spiritual contexts (or anyone who has read and thought deeply about the Book of Job). Whenever people are struck by a life-threatening disaster, their fundamental sense of meaning, order, and security in the world is shattered. Many people express their dilemma in religious terms: questioning the adequacy of divine justice, lamenting their loss of faith, and fearing renewed attack by the powers of evil. Andrea's dream of the fire developing "an organic consciousness" that embodies evil is a clear expression of the deep spiritual anxiety that can be generated by a disaster. So is Nan's first dream of the "demons from Hell" attacking her (in chapter 1). These religiously oriented dreams are not only good diagnostic indicators of the severity of the trauma, but they are also an opening for caregivers to ask some respectful questions about the person's religious background to see if there might be any therapeutic resources in that area of the person's life. A caregiver does not need to share the person's religious belief in order to provide help in reconnecting the person to the healing possibilities of his or her religious tradition.

Mourning

By the end of 2001, just a few months after September 11, millions of people had already made the pilgrimage to Ground Zero to look, marvel, pray, and cry. Discussion had begun in New York and around the country about what kind of memorial should be built on the site. Some people wanted the entire sixteen acres devoted to a monument to the nearly 3,000 dead, many of whose bodies will remain forever buried in the ground below. Other people wanted the site redeveloped for new commercial activity, with the goal of creating new jobs, providing business services, and testifying to the spirit of American enterprise. Many people envisioned new construction that would aspire to the same lofty grandeur as the original 110-story-tall World Trade Center towers. Rudolph Giuliani, in his farewell speech upon stepping down as mayor of New York, called for a "beautiful, soaring" monument to be built. Others, however, have questioned whether we truly honor the memory of those who died by focusing excessive attention on the size of our buildings. I have heard several people quietly admit they never liked the grandiosity and arrogance of the WTC towers; although these people are deeply sympathetic toward the victims of September 11, they nevertheless believe the WTC towers were targeted by terrorists precisely because of the way they symbolize the overweening pride of American capitalism.

The public discussion about what will constitute the most appropriate monument in New York City for the September 11 attack reflects, from a different angle, the same psychological process I have been describing in this book in relation to dreams and nightmares: the yearning to make meaning in a time of uncertainty, fear, and change. Dreaming is one mode by which this meaning-making process operates, a mode that originates in a relatively personal sphere of life. Building monuments is another mode of meaning-making, and one that proceeds in a relatively public sphere of life. What we build on Ground Zero will be a metaphorical expression for what we as a nation are doing in response to the horrible devastation of September 11. The monument will (if it's a good one) function like a powerful collective dream, helping us become more fully aware of what we have suffered and reminding us of the hopes we still have for the future.

Peter Homans, a psychologist and sociologist of religion at the University of Chicago and one of my graduate school mentors, has written perceptively about the psychology of public monuments. Homans calls new attention to Freud's ideas in *Mourning and Melancholia* (1918) regarding the psychological impact of experiences of loss. For Freud the various losses people suffer through their lives, although deeply painful, can have the valuable effect of spurring the development of important new psychological structures. "Mourning" is Freud's term for the process by which this new development occurs, transforming painful grief into a renewed capacity for creative living. Although he devoted most of his analysis to people's emotional responses to the death of a loved one, like a parent or spouse, Freud briefly noted that people could also mourn the loss of abstractions like "liberty" or "one's country."[23] Homans takes this insight of Freud's and uses it to explore the remarkably widespread phenomenon of "symbolic loss" through modern Western history: "Typically, symbolic loss refers to the loss of an attachment to a political ideology or religious creed, or to some aspect or fragment of one, and to the inner work of coming to terms with this kind of loss. In this sense it resembles mourning. However, in the case of symbolic loss the object that is lost is, ordinarily, sociohistorical, cognitive, and

45

collective. The lost object is a symbol or rather a system of symbols and not a person."[24]

For a community of people mourning a symbolic loss, one of the natural means of expressing the group's feelings is to build monuments to that which was lost. "Traditionally, the monument has been the material structure around which both personal and collective mourning have taken place, and it has facilitated that mourning through a process of return and release. The monument 're-presents' a past event and serves as a carrier of memory back through time to that event. After the event has been recollected and reflected upon, memory is released, and one comes back, so to speak, to the present. Through this process, memory of an earlier experience of loss is assuaged and rendered, or rerendered, less stressful."[25]

In his studies of the Vietnam War Memorial in Washington, D.C., and the Holocaust Memorial at Majdanek, Lublin, Poland, Homans has shown that public monuments play a vital role in a community's efforts to recover from terrible losses of both human life and cherished ideals.[26] At their best, monuments stimulate a powerful psychological process within each individual that complements the personal mourning already under way—"the monument is the social complement to mourning, missing in Freud's formulations: it is to the structure of culture what the dream is to the structure of the mind. Mourning and monuments link the past to the present."[27]

If we follow Homans in these ideas about the deep structural connection between dreams and monuments, we come to an important realization regarding the practice of caregiving with people who have been wounded by a collective disaster: Just as much as they should be invited to share and reflect upon their dreams, trauma victims should be encouraged to participate in community efforts to memorialize the disaster. This participation can take many different forms—in the case of September 11, not everyone will be involved in designing and building the monument at the site of the World Trade Center, but each individual has available a wide variety of opportunities to give creative expression to his or her feelings of loss. In the neighborhood where I live (just north of Berkeley, California), spontaneous memorials were constructed at two prominent traffic intersections, one a water fountain at the center of a roundabout intersection and the other a small triangular space formed by metal barriers guiding traffic. Just a few days after September 11, people began bringing a variety of offerings to these two publicly visible spots: candles, flags, flowers, pictures of loved ones, papers written with prayers for peace (very much like the scene outside Trinity Church near Ground Zero). During the evenings people from around the neighborhood would gather in small groups at both places to light the candles, sing, and talk about what was happening. Spontaneous shrines like these appeared in many other parts of the country after September 11, and they testify to the value of creative activity as a means of healing the wounds of collective trauma.

Much like dreaming, monument building in all its variations opens the way to the development of new psychological strength and vitality. I suggest caregivers do as much as they can to encourage and enhance the deep symbolic interplay between dreaming and creating memorials. The combined effect of these two modes of meaning-making can be a powerful aid in helping survivors of a major life crisis come through the mourning process with a renewed capacity for love, hope, and joy.

Essential Bibliography

Browning, Don S. 1991. *A Fundamental Practical Theology: Descriptive and Strategic Proposals.* Minneapolis: Fortress Press.

Bulkeley, Kelly. 1996b. Political Dreaming: Dreams of the 1992 Presidential Election. In *Among All These Dreamers: Essays on*

Dreaming and Modern Society, ed. K. Bulkeley. Albany: State University of New York Press.

———. 2000. *Transforming Dreams: Learning Spiritual Lessons from the Dreams You Never Forget*. New York: John Wiley & Sons.

Domhoff, G. William. 1996. *Finding Meaning in Dreams: A Quantitative Approach*. New York: Plenum.

Homans, Peter. 1989. *The Ability to Mourn: Disillusionment and the Social Origins of Psychoanalysis*. Chicago: University of Chicago Press.

———. 2001. Contemporary Perspectives on Dying, Death, and Bereavement. Paper read at Annual Meeting of the American Academy of Religion, November 16, Denver, Colorado.

———, ed. 2000. *Symbolic Loss: The Ambiguity of Mourning and Memory at Century's End*. Charlottesville: University of Virginia Press.

Siegel, Alan. 1996. Dreams of Firestorm Survivors. In *Trauma and Dreams*, ed. D. Barrett. Cambridge: Harvard University Press.

Sullivan, Kathleen. 1998. *Recurring Dreams: A Journey to Wholeness*. Freedom: The Crossing Press.

Taylor, Jeremy. 1983. *Dream Work*. Mahwah: Paulist Press.

———. 1992. *Where People Fly and Water Runs Uphill*. New York: Warner Books.

Terror Attacks Take Hidden Toll. 2002. *New York Daily News*, 1/20.

Notes

1. Personal communication, 1/1/02.
2. Personal communication, 1/1/02.
3. Personal communication, 12/13/01.
4. Personal communication, 1/21/02.

5. Personal communication, 2/1/02.
6. For more on the philosophical history and contemporary treatment of the notion of *phronesis*, see Browning 1991.
7. Countless people have mentioned how "movie-like" the September 11 attack was, and this is undoubtedly an additional reason for its deep psychological impact.
8. Bulkeley 1996b.
9. Personal communication, 10/31/01.
10. Taylor 1983, 1992. While agreeing with Taylor's basic point, I have been persuaded by Steven Bauman, a student at the Graduate Theological Union, that we need to think more carefully about how we understand and relate to the energies of evil, malevolence, and destruction that emerge in both dreaming and waking life.
11. For information about keeping a dream journal, see Bulkeley 2000, chap. 7.
12. For more on the exploration of recurrent elements as a means of understanding the psychological and spiritual dimensions of dreams, see Sullivan 1998. For more on what recurrent dream elements reveal about the psychological nature of the dreamer, see Domhoff 1996.
13. The panel was organized by Cynthia Pearson, and has continued at the past several ASD conferences.
14. Personal communication, 11/12/01.
15. Personal communication, 12/13/01.
16. I'm echoing the words of William Genet, Director of Police Organization Providing Peer Assistance: "You're still treated with a jaundiced eye if you seek help from the department. The police and firefighters think if you need help, you shouldn't be a firefighter or cop." (Terror Attacks 2002)
17. Terror Attacks 2002.
18. Siegel 1996, 161.
19. Siegel 1996, 163.

20. Siegel 1996, 162.
21. Siegel 1996, 163.
22. Siegel 1996, 163.
23. Homans 2000, 19–22.
24. Homans 2000, 20.
25. Homans 2000, 22.
26. Homans 2001.
27. Homans 1989, 258.

3. The Fear of New Dangers

More Terrorist Attacks?

The immediate response to an unexpected disaster like the September 11 terrorist attack is, of course, extreme fear. In a time of crisis everyone feels anxious, defensive, and hypervigilant toward any possible danger or threat. I had a brief encounter with that kind of intense anxiety a few days after September 11, when I was going for a midday run in Tilden Park, in the hills above my house. I had a terrible head cold at the time, and while I chugged along I couldn't help coughing, snuffling, and spitting rather profusely. As I passed a lone car parked near the roadside, the man inside suddenly threw open his door and shouted, "Don't spit on my car!"

I stopped in surprise, turned around, and said, "What are you talking about? I didn't do anything to your car."

The man glared at me for a moment, and then snarled, "*I don't like people spitting near my car!*"

Now in those shocked, confused, surrealistic days following September 11, I felt just as edgy as everyone else, and initially I flared with anger at the man and almost yelled back something like, "Well, what if I *did* spit on your car? You gonna do anything about it?" Then the thought flashed through my mind that maybe I should just be sarcastic and say, "That's right, I'm a terrorist with nuclear spitballs and I'm aiming them at *your car!*"

In the end, I decided simply to let it go.

"Hey, chill out," I said to him.

I turned away and continued on my run (with all senses alert to the possibility that the guy still might come after me).

A fearful self-protectiveness is a natural reaction to trauma. It is like the hard scab that covers a raw wound, shielding it from further damage and giving it a chance to heal. In time the scab can be sloughed off, the defensive posture relaxed, and openness to the world restored. The art of caregiving lies in knowing when to respect the emotional scab of self-protective anxiety and when to promote the transition back to openness, health, and creative living. It is important to remember, however, that a heightened degree of vigilance toward potential dangers will always remain for people who have suffered through a terrible disaster, just as an especially bad cut to the skin will always leave a scar. Even after the self-protective scab is gone and the healing work is done, a deep psychological or physical wound fundamentally *changes* a person in ways that remain throughout life. This means that practical efforts at caregiving should not be misled by the expectation that people's suffering can be completely eliminated or eradicated from their lives. Most people who experience a severe trauma will readily confess that the pain is always with them, the memories of the event always vivid, the fear of new threats always fresh. For these people, healing does not mean the abolishment of their suffering. Rather, it means developing new abilities to continue living a vital and creative life, *with those deep psychological wounds now and forever an integral part of themselves.*

In this chapter I look at a set of dreams reflecting the development of new sensitivities to external danger, a development that I believe marks an important moment in the process of growing beyond a traumatic event. Current scientific research on the evolutionary benefits of human dreaming suggests that a major function of dreams is to enhance our abilities to identify and defend against potential threats in the waking environment. Antti

Revonsuo, a neuroscientist working in Finland, has made a persuasive argument that dreaming works to simulate potential threats in our waking world, with the beneficial result that we are better prepared to face such threats when they actually arise in waking life.[1] As evidence of this "threat simulation" function, Revonsuo points to the vivid realism of dreaming, its frequent portrayal of frightening threats, and its tendency to be triggered into heightened activation by actual experiences of physical danger (as occurs with PTSD nightmares). Revonsuo's research underscores the importance for caregivers of looking to dreams for expressions of basic survival skills that remain active despite the fear, confusion, and suffering caused by an unexpected catastrophe. Following this line of thinking, I suggest that many of the frightening nightmares people experience in the aftermath of a sudden disaster are evidence not only of fear, weakness, and vulnerability, but also of enduring strength and vitality. In Revonsuo's terms, post-traumatic dreams display the basic forces of life working vigorously to deal with the most pressing challenges of the individual's external environment. Understood in this way, dreams become a valuable ally in caregiving practice because they have the potential to bring to conscious awareness a fuller recognition of the deep, powerful strengths that remain alive within people.

In the days immediately following September 11, many people said they were particularly shocked by the fact that a violent, warlike attack had been made "on our own soil," right here within the geographic boundaries of the United States. In recent years American soldiers have been involved in various battles in other countries around the world, but not since the December 7, 1941, attack on Pearl Harbor have our national boundaries been violated in such a flagrant and outrageous way. Indeed, even Pearl Harbor pales in comparison to the September 11 attack. December 7, "the day that will live in infamy," involved horrible death and destruction, but the violence was primarily aimed at and suffered by military personnel. September 11, by contrast, was an indiscriminate attack aimed at *all* Americans, civilians and soldiers alike. Any one of us could have been in one of those buildings or on one of those planes. And while Pearl Harbor was a relatively small outpost on the farthest outskirts of the nation, the World Trade Center and the Pentagon lay in the very heart of the country's economic and political capitals. For all these reasons, many Americans experienced September 11 as a shocking violation of their personal sense of safety and security.

In this regard, the better source of comparative information is not from studies of PTSD in Vietnam veterans, but from clinical research on victims of domestic violence. I will discuss that sphere of research and its implications for caregivers once we have examined a new set of dreams relating to September 11. These dreams reflect a theme I found in nearly every dream I gathered: a fearful realization that terrorism, warfare, and anti-American violence have come shockingly "close to home." These dreams are a kind of mirror opposite of the dreams discussed earlier (particularly Melissa's in chapter 1 and Julie's in chapter 2). Rather than imaginatively going *to* the World Trade Center, these people find themselves dreaming of the September 11 attacks coming to *them*, in the form of violent threats against their actual geographic homes. For example, a young man ("Bill") who was born and raised in the San Francisco Bay Area, had this dream in early November:

I was watching the news and the television suddenly turned off. Then it turned on again. The news came on and said that the Afghans had dropped a bomb in the San Francisco Bay and they were going to bomb again within the next few days. I tried to escape the Bay Area but I couldn't because all the roads were jammed.[2]

Even though he lives 3,000 miles away from Ground Zero, and a further several thousand miles away from the military action in

Afghanistan, Bill said he had numerous dreams of terrorists to go along with this dream of an Afghan bomb dropped in the center of his home area. Such dreams show how personally impacted Bill was by September 11, despite being so physically distant from it. In his dream the war is *right here, right now*—it is part of his life, an inescapable reality. Here is perhaps the plainest possible illustration of Revonsuo's "threat simulation" function. After September 11, Bill (like every other American) realized he was vulnerable to a kind of deadly attack he had never before thought possible. As a consequence, his dreaming imagination created a vivid simulation of what would happen if the same kind of attack struck *him*. In neuropsychological terms, this kind of dream contributes to Bill's adaptive fitness by rehearsing various survival strategies and fine-tuning the efficiency of the various cognitive processes that would be involved in his responding to an actual waking-world threat. In dreams like this, "Forewarned is forearmed" is the operating principle.

"Ann," a college student who grew up in the Hawaiian islands and now goes to school there, had two dream fragments that came on the night of September 11, after she finally turned off the TV and went to sleep:

I was riding a car through a scenic route in the islands, and a woman's voice who sounded like my mother's voice told me to take pictures of the sky. It was filled with black smoke with patches of blue skies and white clouds and the moon was high above but it was not night. I was fascinated with a curiosity of what was going on. I began to take pictures of certain parts of the sky. Each time I snapped a picture some would come out clear and others would be pitch black. I felt myself seem very confused of why this was happening to the pictures I took.

The next thing I knew my family and I drove around Oahu. We were camping in a field of red dirt with sugar cane and pineapple all around. Me and somebody (I can't remember who) went walking up a long road to a store to get something. When walking back, the ground shook and I could see a fireball in the distance. Then about 10–15 mete-ors hit the island. One big one hit the campsite where my family was. I was yelling No! No! No! and filled up with fear and pain. I ran as fast as I could to the area. The only thing left was a big ditch with black ashes all around. I was filled with sadness and pain. Then I woke up with fear and couldn't believe what I dreamed.[3]

Ann directly connected her dream to the emotional turmoil she felt that day. "Having seen and heard the news of the terror-ist attack the day before was shocking, unbelievable, but also heartbreaking for me. Going to bed late with the television still showing the images of the WTC tragedy probably triggered my dreams." Even though Ann was as physically far removed as an American could be from the terrorist attacks, the psychological impact on her was sharp and intense. Her two dream fragments expressed her fear that what happened on September 11 posed a direct and personal threat to her family, her home, and herself. Although there are hints of strength here—the guidance from the mother-like voice, the power of her own curiosity, the fertility of the land—the overall tenor of the dream is an alarming sense of immediate personal danger.

As I gathered dreams following September 11, I heard people from one end of the country to the other having dreams like this, horrifying visions of families and homes being bombed, attacked, and caught up in sudden violence and war-fare. In its dreaming imagination, the whole nation became Ground Zero.

One more example of this kind of dream comes from another corner of the United States, far removed from the geo-graphic sites of the September 11 attack. "Terry" is a college stu-dent who grew up in Anchorage, Alaska, and is now attending school in Washington state. A month after the attack she had this dream, which she said was "very disturbing":

I was at home in Anchorage with my family. We were at my house when we started to hear big booms. We looked out and saw helicopters and bombs being dropped. We braced ourselves as a fierce wind went through the house (I guess that was the result of a bomb). Being that it was a dream, our house was still standing after the bombs were dropped but I was running around telling my family that we had to get out of there. We started to go out the back door, but there was a man in uniform outside asking if him and his troops could come in. I was hesitant to say yes but did. And then there was this little boy (I don't know where he came from) that knew the future. All he said was "Saddam Hussein will win" in a loud voice. Everyone was frightened. Then the ghost of the little boy and Samuel L. Jackson (I don't know how he appeared either) appeared. They were saying good-bye to each other. Then they disappeared. It was all very strange....[4]

Like the dreams of Ann and Bill, Terry's dream portrays a violent attack on her home that directly threatens her family. At one level, her dream is a clear instance of a personal symbol. Just a few days earlier she had flown from Anchorage to school, and she was staying in a new apartment that felt strange and unsettled. In this regard Terry's dream symbolizes her general longing for home and her fearful awareness that she is in a new and potentially dangerous living place.

At another level, the exploding bombs and ferocious winds in Terry's dream are apt metaphors for the tremendous emotional impact of the terrorist attack on people all over the country. For many Americans the most jarring reminder of the incredible changes wrought by September 11 was the prominent positioning of National Guard troops at airports, government buildings, major bridges, and national monuments. Terry's dream expresses a widely shared ambivalence about the military mobilization, and I find it intriguing that the specific imagery of her dream— uniformed soldiers asking to stay in her house—portrays the exact conflict addressed by the Third Amendment to the U.S.

Constitution: "No Soldier shall, in time of peace be quartered in any house, without the consent of the Owner, nor in time of war, but in a manner to be prescribed by law." Putting aside the Amendment's political and legal aspects, the deeper psychological issue here is how to balance freedom and security in our lives. Where should the line be drawn between the sovereignty of one's private self and the need to sacrifice some of that privacy in the cause of greater communal safety? A traumatizing event like September 11 radically shifts our feelings about such matters, and people naturally feel a sense of uncertainty and disorientation as they struggle to determine what, following the trauma, is an appropriate level of defensive preparedness for possible future threats at both the personal and collective level. For Terry, her dream actions ("I was hesitant to say yes but I did") closely parallels her waking beliefs about the U.S. military response to September 11: "I feel that they are an undesirable but necessary precaution to regaining our nation's freedom."[5]

Terry's dream contains some unusual features that merit closer attention. The inexplicable appearance of the little boy who knows the future, his sudden transformation into a ghost, the equally inexplicable appearance of the actor Samuel L. Jackson, and their final disappearance—this whole final scene of the dream is dramatically different from the earlier scene in Terry's house. Although dreams have a reputation for being totally bizarre and fantastical, most dreams are in fact rather straightforward portrayals of events that either have happened or could plausibly happen in the dreamer's ordinary waking life. We usually dream about people we know, places we live, and things we do in ordinary waking life. This is important to remember when considering those dreams in which truly unusual, extraordinary elements are included. Whatever else you think about dreams, it can't be denied that the dreaming imagination has nearly infinite creative abilities at its disposal—dreams can portray us with anyone, in any place, doing practically anything.

The question, then, is why, given the dreaming imagination's usual preference for images from ordinary life, does a particular dream (like Terry's) go to the trouble of creating such strikingly unusual and unrealistic elements?

If some part of a dream is a "counterfactual," that is, a sharp deviation from the normal realities of the dreamer's waking world, I like to examine that element very carefully to see if it may be conveying something of importance and value to the dreamer's conscious awareness. In response to my questions, Terry said she felt the strange little boy was expressing her own deepest fears, and his ability to foresee the future reflects her anxious anticipation of being directly involved in future violence generated by the "war on terrorism" (after Afghanistan, Saddam Hussein's regime in Iraq was the most frequently mentioned target of possible U.S. military action). Understood in this light, the boy gives voice to a mysterious but powerful capacity *within Terry* for discerning future danger, a capacity that has been activated by the awful events of September 11 and is now scanning her world for possible threats. Regarding Samuel L. Jackson, Terry commented that she likes the strong, competent characters he usually plays in his movies. These are the very qualities Terry is seeking in herself and in her country's leaders, and the fact that the boy and Jackson disappear at the very end of her dream leaves her with troubling questions when she wakes up: Where did they go? What does it mean that the boy "died"? Was he right about Saddam Hussein?

Dreams do not end randomly. Unless they are artificially interrupted by an alarm clock, dreams usually come to a conclusion at a very particular point, and often it's right *then* that the dreamer wakes up, with those final images vivid and clear in his or her mind. The effect of this is to implant the dream quite dramatically in conscious awareness, compelling the individual to think (for a few moments at least) about what he or she was just experiencing. I see the process as a kind of psychological "call and response": the dream ends with a question, and it's the job of waking consciousness to carry that question forward and try to find an answer to it. Terry's dream illustrates this dynamic relationship by ending at the precise moment of the disappearance of the boy and Jackson, thereby prompting her to consider deeply important questions about the uncertainties of the future—questions that many other emotionally distraught Americans were asking themselves in the days and weeks following September 11.

What Nan Feared Most

Let's go back to the first four dreams Nan had after her car accident. You might expect, following the idea that after a trauma people become hypervigilant toward future threats, that Nan would be dreaming constantly of car crashes. But that turns out not to be the case. In fact, none of Nan's dreams in the entire six months following her accident had any direct reference to cars or crashes of any kind. If you simply read the written text of her dreams, without any additional knowledge of her life or personal circumstances, you would have to be an incredibly lucky guesser to be able to say what had happened to her. Nevertheless, Nan's dreams following the accident were filled with fear, anxiety, and vulnerability. If she's not overtly worried about future car accidents, what is she so scared of?

Recall the distressing scenarios in her initial four dreams:

1. She is threatened by the curtains surrounding her hospital bed, which are transforming themselves into "creatures like demons from Hell."

2. She is covered in shit, can't see, and has lost her baby; darts strike her and she doesn't know where they are coming from.

3. She is in a "dark flat with other abandoned children."

4. She finds a young woman lying on the white-tiled floor of a shower, bleeding, the life ebbing out of her; the young woman asks Nan for help, but Nan knows she will not die.

As different as these four dreams are from each other, they all revolve around a theme that (following the suggestions of psychologist Deirdre Barrett and content analysis researcher G. William Domhoff) I would term "problematic nurturance." In the first dream Nan is mortally frightened by a setting (the hospital) that is devoted to caring for her. In the second dream Nan is in a mothering position, but everything about her efforts to care for the baby goes wrong (she never refers to the baby as he or she, only as "it"), and at the end of the dream she can't protect herself against the darts. The third dream places Nan in the child's position, abandoned with the other helpless women in the hospital ward—no one is there to care for them. And in the fourth dream the young woman seems to be dying, but Nan makes no move to help her because she knows the young woman will survive. When Nan awoke she immediately associated the young woman's bleeding to a first menstruation—the initiation of a woman's ability to bring new life into being, and the first sign of potential motherhood. This close juxtaposition of death and new life in her fourth dream parallels the juxtaposition of caring and not caring in the previous three other dreams. Already we can begin to see the outline of what Nan is most worried about: not future car crashes, but something to do with caring, mothering, protecting, and nurturing.

This theme of problematic nurturance is further illustrated in Nan's next two dreams.

5. Dreamed I wasn't getting my work done it looked clean, but I had only feed kids once—they were OK with it but I knew I wasn't able to do it the way I should. I'm not doing what I should.

6. Phil had moved back in, again, he was uninvited back in the house doing trivial things and things I didn't like...making small almost unseeable designs on pages, spending all his energy on the inconsequential and ignoring me..us..., pretending to be a foreign professor and raking students over the coals thinking it was a lark, and yet I felt he was there to stay and maybe I had to surrender for my kid's sake and then I would be old and too vulnerable to make him leave..I would have to endure his insertion into my life. a loss of freedom and independence.

"Phil" is Nan's ex-husband, whom she had divorced more than a dozen years earlier. They had four children together, all grown by now, and while Nan and Phil were cordial at family gatherings they had little contact otherwise. In her sixth dream, however, he's right back in her life, bothering her with his selfish and impulsive behavior. Nan feels powerless to stop him, and the crucial emotional message comes right at the end of the dream: She is feeling "old and vulnerable" and fears "a loss of freedom and independence."

When I asked Nan about this part of her dream, she said it was a very accurate description of her emotional concerns immediately following the accident, and she said it felt directly related to her second dream. That dream expressed her terrible distress at finding herself warehoused in a hospital ward with a bunch of "old women," all of whom were there for hip replacement surgery (a common procedure for aging women). None of them received more than a couple of visitors during their hospital stay, and Nan could tell they were lonely. Lying in her own hospital bed day after day, Nan became deeply uncomfortable in this bleak setting, and she could not help thinking, "This is what I have to look forward to."[6]

Prior to her accident, Nan did not feel herself to be an elderly person—on the contrary, she was training for a new career in the ministry, and she looked forward to many new activities and challenges in the future. But the car accident threatened all of that. Suddenly she was in danger of dying, totally dependent on the care of others, and facing the possibility of never recovering her full health and strength. Even worse, she began to worry that the accident might trigger an early onset of dementia. Nan's mother had suffered from Alzheimer's disease before her death, and as Nan struggled with memory problems following her accident she was acutely aware that a similar fate might be in store for her.

In her dreams Nan has trouble caring for others, and she is uncared for herself. She expresses deep concern about her capacities as a mother and also about her own needs to be nurtured and protected. Taking these six dreams as a whole, it becomes clear that Nan's great fear in the future is becoming a helpless, mentally vacant old woman. This fear does not refer directly to her car accident, the original cause of her current crisis. Rather, her greatest fear focuses on a potential future consequence of the original event. Her dreams portray what she is afraid will happen to her as a result of the accident. As we saw in the previous section with Terry's dream, which prompted her to think about future dangers to the country, the healing function of Nan's dreams is to focus her conscious awareness on the future. Nan's dreams reveal the most pressing challenges she is facing in the aftermath of her car accident, and as disturbing and nightmarish as her dreams may be, they are part of a deeply powerful process (both psychological and spiritual in nature) that is working to concentrate her emotional energies on responding to those threats and renewing her sense of health, vitality, and hopefulness in the world.

Safe Spaces

As I mentioned in chapter 1, a great deal of research has been conducted in recent years on the dreams and nightmares of people who have suffered physical or sexual abuse in the home. As with the Vietnam veterans, victims of domestic violence almost always report increased levels of sleep disruption, nightmares, and night terrors.[7] They have frequent dreams of explicit violence and sexual assaults, and the characters of their dreams include a variety of threatening humans, animals, and supernatural creatures. But in surprising contrast to the studies on PTSD nightmares among Vietnam vets, the dreams of abuse victims do *not* seem to portray exact recreations of the traumatizing experience. Kathryn Belicki and Marion Cuddy have done important research on the multiple effects of sexual abuse on dreaming, and they say, "Overall, what is perhaps most interesting in these findings was that the nightmares typically did not replay the actual abusive event....What these nightmares seemed to portray was the emotional reality of the event."[8] This certainly seems true of all the dreams we have discussed so far. Nan, Terry, the people affected by September 11, they all experienced dreams that gave vivid expression to the deep emotional impact of whatever crisis had struck them. The dreams portrayed a painfully heightened sense of vulnerability in which previously safe personal spaces—the body, the home, the nation—had been violated by violence and destruction, and terrible new dangers loomed in the future.

Belicki and Cuddy also examined various approaches to the clinical treatment of abuse victims, and they found that talking with people about their dreams is a valuable way of promoting and enriching the therapeutic relationship. For example, Cuddy worked with a woman ("Victoria") who suffered sexual abuse at the hands of her brother when she was a teenager. Victoria never told anyone about what happened to her, but fifty-five years later, after several suicide attempts and a long period of deep depression, she was brought to Cuddy's care in a hospital psychiatric ward. Over several months Victoria and Cuddy developed a mutual sense of trust, fostered in large part by their detailed discussion of her dreams and nightmares. Cuddy notes a remarkable evolution in one of the themes of Victoria's dreams as their therapeutic work proceeded:

Early in therapy she [Victoria] had a dream about being carried into an ambulance and conveyed to a hospital. [She was, in fact, committed to the hospital involuntarily.] There were other dreams in which she was carried into a vehicle. Later, she progressed to actively entering a vehicle albeit in the capacity of a passenger. Then, she had a dream in which she found herself driving the car but from the passenger's side; finally, she graduated to being the driver of a car and quickly following this was a series of dreams in which she adopted extremely active roles. Her progress in dreams predated any signs of such empowerment in her real life. We have similarly observed, with many others, that often changes first appear in dreams and then later emerge in waking behavior. The dream permits the person to do a trial run of behavior or attitude and examine its consequences.[9]

The last sentence echoes the research of Antti Revonsuo mentioned earlier, especially his notion of dreams as "perceptually and behaviorally realistic rehearsals"[10] of the kinds of basic survival skills necessary to deal with real waking world dangers. Cuddy and Belicki provide clinical evidence for the same essential claim, that dreaming provides an imaginal space in which people can develop better ways of dealing with the major threats confronting them in their current waking lives.

The changes in Victoria's dream life through the course of her therapy with Cuddy bears striking similarities to the dreams of a patient of Medard Boss, the Swiss psychoanalyst who was trained in Freudian clinical practice, worked for ten years with Jung in Zurich, and went on to develop a highly influential mode of philosophy he called "existential psychoanalysis." In his book *The Analysis of Dreams*, Boss recounts the story of an engineer in his forties who came to Boss for psychotherapy because of depression and sexual impotence.[11] The engineer told Boss he had never dreamed once in his entire life, but just two days before their first session he actually did remember a dream.[12] In this dream the engineer is imprisoned in a dungeon whose bars are made of mathematical signs and numbers. After the analysis got started, the engineer began bringing new dreams to every session. Boss noticed that during the first six and a half months the engineer dreamed only of machines, cars, planes, and electronic devices. Then, for the first time, he dreamed of a living thing—a potted plant. Four months later the engineer began dreaming of insects, all of them dangerous and harmful. After that he dreamed for a time of toads, frogs, and snakes. The first mammal to appear in the engineer's dream was a mouse, which scurried down a mouse hole the instant it was seen. Next were dreams of pigs, then of lions and horses. After two years of analysis the engineer finally dreamed of a human being. In that dream he discovered a giant, unconscious woman, in a long, blood-red dress, trapped under an ice-covered pond; terrified, he ran for help. Six months later, the engineer dreamed that he was dancing at a party with a vibrant woman dressed in a similar blood-red outfit, and they fell in passionate love with each other. Boss reports that the engineer's depression had begun disappearing by the time of the potted plant dream, and his sexual potency had returned when he began dreaming of lions and horses.

The engineer's dreams, like the dreams of Cuddy's patient, Victoria, illustrate the point I made earlier in the chapter about the powerful role of dreaming in the healing process. To repeat and emphasize Cuddy and Belicki's key insight, what happens in dreams is often *ahead* of what is happening psychologically in people's current waking lives. Dreams look toward the future of the healing—they anticipate the changes to come, and they envision new possibilities for active, energetic living. The engineer's dreams portray this process with an evolutionary metaphor, correlating his personal growth with the biological emergence of increasingly complex life forms. Victoria's dreams make use of a car metaphor, with a gradual transformation of her status from a powerless passenger to an active driver. This particular metaphor makes good sense given the circumstances surrounding Victoria's hospitalization.

The two case studies offer unusually clear illustrations of the transformations that can occur in people's dreams as they struggle to overcome severe psychological and spiritual difficulties. I would not expect every series of dreams to display the healing process with such symbolic eloquence. In most cases the process is much messier, with regressions, setbacks, and long periods of seeming stagnation. But here again, Cuddy and Belicki's point is worth highlighting. Over time, and with the support of skilled caregivers, people's dreams can provide them with a safe, private, imaginative arena in which to confront their suffering, mourn their losses, and actively seek new opportunities for future growth. It is not simply that the dreams are reflecting the healing process, as a kind of diagnostic indicator of psychological process. Rather, *dreaming is the healing process itself*—it is a vital means by which we bind up our wounded spirits and rekindle our hopes for the future.

Essential Bibliography

Belicki, Kathryn, & Marion Cuddy. 1996. Identifying Sexual Trauma Histories from Patterns of Sleep and Dreams. In *Trauma and Dreams*, ed. D. Barrett. Cambridge: Harvard University Press.

Boss, Medard. 1958. *The Analysis of Dreams*. New York: Philosophical Library.

Cuddy, Marion, & Kathryn Belicki. 1996. The 55-Year Secret: Using Nightmares to Facilitate Psychotherapy in a Case of

Childhood Sexual Abuse. In *Among All These Dreamers: Essays on Dreaming and Modern Society*, ed. K. Bulkeley. Albany: State University of New York Press.

Revonsuo, Antti. 2000. The Reinterpretation of Dreams: An Evolutionary Hypothesis of the Function of Dreaming. *Behavioral and Brain Sciences* 23 (6).

White-Lewis, Jane. 2001. Reflecting on a Dream in Jungian Analytic Practice. In *Dreams: A Reader on the Religious, Cultural, and Psychological Dimensions of Dreaming*, ed. K. Bulkeley. New York: Palgrave.

Notes

1. Revonsuo 2000.
2. Personal communication, 11/11/01.
3. Personal communication, 12/5/01.
4. Personal communication, 11/25/01.
5. Personal communication, 11/30/01.
6. Personal communication, 6/1/02.
7. Belicki & Cuddy 1996, 54.
8. Belicki & Cuddy 1996, 53.
9. Cuddy & Belicki, 1996, 28.
10. Revonsuo 2000.
11. Boss 1958.
12. For more on "first dreams" and their significance for clinical practice, see White-Lewis 2001.

4. Flying and Falling

The Magic and Peril of Flying

A curious thing I have noticed in several years of studying the dream beliefs and practices of various cultural traditions is that the airplane is one of the first elements of the "modern world" to enter into the dreaming imaginations of people living in non-Western, pre-modern communities. Among the many technological marvels that have been abruptly introduced to (or forced upon) the indigenous peoples of the Americas, Oceania, Africa, and other parts of the world, the airplane has made an especially strong psychological impact, as evidenced by these people's dreams. For example, anthropologist Robert Tonkinson examined the complex reactions of Australian Aborigines to their initial encounters with Western technology, and he found that

> Aboriginal conceptions of the dream-spirit have been influenced by contact with "whites." Crayon drawings made by Aborigines of *badundjari* [the spirits that leave the body during sleep and fly off on various adventures] sometimes resemble aircraft, and vehicles said to be used by *badundjari* to transport others are depicted as airplanes, complete with wings, tail, windows and headlights, but with sacred boards [a traditional object of spiritual force], not propellers or jets, supplying the power source. The Aborigines usually insist that the dream-spirits had these types of vehicle before the Europeans invented them.[1]

Similar effects have been recorded among indigenous communities throughout the Americas, where people's dreams have been dramatically impacted by the sudden and often violent encounter with the airplanes, cars, guns, radios, and other technological wonders possessed by white settlers.[2] According to anthropologist Thomas Gregor, the Mehinaku people of the Brazilian rain forest have frequent dreams of whites and their technology—highly negative dreams that reflect the damaging effects on their culture of contact with the modern world. The Mehinaku suffered many terrible outbreaks of measles and other infectious diseases brought by outsiders, and their dreams associated these diseases with white people generally, as in this dream reported by Gregor:

At the post [government office and trading center] a plane landed. Many, many passengers got off. It seemed as if there was a village in the plane. I was very frightened of them and the things they carried. I was afraid they would bring a disease to the village, the white man's "witchcraft."[3]

Other Mehinaku dreams intensified this connection of airplanes and danger to the community:

We went to the place where the canoe was moored. A plane came overhead and broke in the sky. It crashed in the water and everything caught on fire. The gasoline floated on the water. My mother caught on fire.[4]

These negatively toned airplane dreams are only part of the story, however. All around the world, dreams of airplanes draw symbolic power from their association with another cross-cultural dream theme, one that is the conceptual opposite of falling: *flying*. For ages, long before the invention of airplanes, humans have dreamed of flying, and these dreams have in most cultures been revered and celebrated as sacred experiences.[5] People today often describe their flying dreams as the most joyful dream experiences they have ever had, and they lament the fact that they used to have more such dreams in childhood. This is the other half of the universal fascination with airplanes: Planes enable us to do in physical reality what we most enjoy doing in our dreams. This is why Australian Aborigines and other indigenous traditions around the world have incorporated images of airplanes into their religious iconography. The airplane symbolizes a deeply spiritual yearning for freedom, liberation, and transcendence, a yearning that has long been part of the human imagination.

I offer this discussion of cross-cultural examples of airplane dreams as a symbolic and metaphorical context in which to consider the similar dreams of people in contemporary American society. Commercial airplane crashes are a sadly regular feature of modern life, and I will offer some practical guidelines for caregivers who are working with people affected by a plane crash. Dreams offer a remarkably clear insight into the emotional turmoil caused by such an experience, and they can reveal important clues about where the healing process is going. These days, a few points about airplane dreams should probably be part of any kind of training program for caregivers—there were many disastrous plane crashes before September 11, and there are bound to be many more in the future.

Crashing Planes

Without a doubt one of the biggest reasons why the September 11 terrorist attack had such a profound emotional impact on the national psyche was that it involved commercial airplanes. We do not know if the perpetrators explicitly intended this, but the terrorizing effect of their attack was greatly magnified by the diabolical use of ordinary commercial planes as flying bombs.[6] Although millions of Americans take trips on airplanes every year, a significant percentage of those people are deeply frightened of the experience, and many more people are at least moderately uncomfortable with the idea of being enclosed for hours at a time in a small metal cylinder 30,000 feet above the ground. This widespread fear of air travel is abundantly evident in people's dream lives, where dreams of flying on planes that are falling, out of control, and/or about to crash are remarkably common among people in contemporary society.[7] In these dreams, airplanes serve as a kind of symbol of life in modern America: the promise of freedom and the power of technology are combined with a fear of going too fast, losing control, falling to the ground, crashing, exploding….In all these ways, airplane dreams serve as an ideal metaphor to express people's feelings about the direction and speed of their lives in the modern world, the nature of their "loftiest aspirations" and "highest aims," and the difficulty in reaching their chosen destinations. Now, after September 11, nightmares of plane crashes have become even more widespread as people's inherent fear of air travel finds horrifying confirmation in the real world.

The novelist Jonathan Franzen, writing in the "Talk of the Town" section of the first *New Yorker* magazine issue following the terrorist attack (9/24/01), described his own history with airplane dreams:

The one recurring nightmare I've had for many years is about the end of the world, and it goes like this. In a crowded, modern cityscape not unlike lower Manhattan, I'm flying a jetliner down an avenue where everything is wrong. It seems impossible that the buildings to either side of me won't shear my wings off, impossible that I can keep the plane aloft while moving at such a low speed. The way is always blocked, but somehow I manage to turn a sharp corner or to pilot the plane beneath an overpass, only to confront a skyscraper so high that I would have to rise vertically to clear it. As I pull the plane into a dismayingly shallow climb, the skyscraper looms and rushes forward to meet me, and I wake up, with unspeakable relief, in my ordinary bed.

Last Tuesday there was no awakening.[8]

The fearfulness of dreams like Franzen's derives in large part from the way the dreams generate a sickeningly realistic sensation of *falling*. Franzen mentions how extremely relieved he felt when he woke up, and many people who have such dreams experience the same "carryover" effect, by which the intense emotionality of the dream crosses over into the waking state. In this regard I see airplane dreams as similar to other typical dreams, like falling off a cliff or a building, or falling into a deep pit, hole, or chasm. The connecting thread in all these dreams is the strong visceral feeling of helplessly going *down*—losing all support or grounding, becoming caught in the implacable clutches of gravity, plunging toward almost certain death—and then suddenly waking up, with that awful feeling alarmingly fresh and vivid in mind, often intermingled (as in Franzen's case) with an equally intense feeling of relief that "it was only a dream." Few other types of dreams hit people with such intense physical power and unforgettable vividness.[9] It is an easy step, metaphorically speaking, for the dreaming imagination to connect the falling theme with airplane imagery and produce a distinctly modern type of nightmare.

The sense of bizarre horror found in many plane crash dreams is illustrated in the dream of "Neil," a fifty-one-year-old cellular telephone repair technician from Indiana, who had this dream on October 7, about a month after the terrorist attack:

I was standing in a house looking out of the window on a snowy field. It was dark outside but the area seemed to be lit with a subtle light. A passenger jet airplane touched down in the field and skidded along on its belly from my left to right. There was a body of water on the right and the plane tore off its landing gear and part of its belly on the water's edge. The plane slipped into the water tail-up with only the tail section above the water. I was in the plane—the luggage, seats, people were piled into the tail. It was dark and the floor was slanted up. I tried to stand and as I did—a machine gun opened up—the noise was deafening—I could see the muzzle-blasts. Then I was behind the person firing the gun looking down the aisle—I jumped at the place that I had seen the gun. No one was there. The emergency lights came on along the floor of the plane and I could see people moving about. [Then] I was outside the plane, standing on the tail section of the plane banging on the metal hull to let the people inside know that I knew that they were there and not to worry. Other people began to arrive and rescue vehicles came. Men were on the tail section with hammers cutting off rivets to open a hole in the hull. I was then a ways off watching the scene.[10]

Neil made a special point of noting what he called a "strange juxtaposition" in the plane's positioning in his dream. The plane's appearance on the outside—its front down in the water, its tail section up in the air—was the opposite from its appearance on the inside—Neil is standing in the back of the plane, looking upward toward the cockpit. The whole experience was extremely strange and disturbing, and Neil said, "This dream left me agitated from a sound sleep. I laid awake and thought about it for some time. Didn't really go back to sleep that night. Images are yet very clear and I remember a great anguish associated with this dream as I lay thinking about it....This dream is so completely different from those I usually experience that I can only assume that it relates to the events of 9/11."[11]

Here again we come up against the question of how to interpret unusual, bizarre phenomena in dreams. Dreams involving so many sudden shifts in the dreamer's point of view are quite rare (Neil said, "I cannot remember another dream that had this type of change in perspective"), although they happen often enough to attract people's attention when they do occur. One explanation commonly given for such sudden perspective shifts in dreams is that they are nothing more than the nonsensical effects of random surges of neurological activity in the brain during REM sleep.[12] Advocates of this explanation take a skeptical view of dream interpretation generally, questioning whether the interpretation of dreams is any more legitimate than imagining shapes in the clouds, that is, imposing meaning on something that is inherently meaningless. Although I certainly agree that a self-critical skepticism is an essential quality in the practice of dream interpretation (as we discussed in the introduction), I do not agree with the automatic, *a priori* dismissal of any dream element as inherently meaningless or nonsensical. A given dream element may be richly significant, or it may be trivial and unremarkable. The only way to tell is by examining it and reflecting carefully about its place in the broader context of the dream as a whole. Indeed, I have often found that it is precisely the strangest and most bizarre elements of a dream that offer the most significant personal insights for the dreamer's waking life.

In the case of Neil's dream, his clear sense was that the strangely shifting perspectives in his dream were related to his feelings about September 11. When I asked him if he could describe in greater detail his emotional reactions following the terrorist attack, he said he was especially moved by the news stories of the rescue workers going into extremely dangerous situations and risking their lives to help and save others trapped in the WTC ruins. A deeply spiritual man who grew up as a Catholic and now follows both Christian and Buddhist teachings, Neil said, "I sense the presence of God in these moments, a human being human without sense of self. I admit that I have cried at these stories."[13] (Here we see a good example of the public veneration and idealization of the rescue workers, which we discussed from the rescue workers' perspective in chapter 2.) In the aftermath of September 11, Neil found himself evaluating his own beliefs and behaviors, asking himself if there was anything he could do to help people overcome the anger, hatred, and fear that was fueling such horrific violence all over the world. Neil's dream played a key role in this process of self-reflection because he saw the sudden shifts from detached observer to active participant and helper to detached observer again as a symbolic expression of his own

halting efforts to "get involved," to become more active in helping people in the post–September 11 world rather than passively
watching everything fall to pieces without lifting a hand to help.
So one major current of feeling in Neil's reaction to September 11
comes through clearly in the shifting perspectives of his dream,
which no longer looks so "bizarre" now that we can see how the
different points of view metaphorically express the different possibilities he was considering in his personal response to the terrorist attack.

But there's still more going on—like a psychic version of a
Chinese box, Neil's dream contains shifts within shifts within
shifts. In the middle scene, when he suddenly finds himself inside
the plane, the up–down orientation has changed, and he's back in
the rear of the plane with the people, luggage, and seats piled up
behind him; in contrast to the external perspective, he is now
looking up the aisle toward the plane's cockpit, and more specifically toward a machine gun pointing at him and the other passengers. This is an especially intense moment of the dream, when the
machine gun opens fire with a "deafening" noise and Neil's vision
focuses on the "muzzle-blast." Here Neil's perspective abruptly
changes once more, so that now he's behind the person firing the
gun. Neil jumps at the gun, but suddenly no one is there.

What is going on in this rapid sequence of events? Several
things. The reversal of the up–down orientation of the plane
expresses at one level Neil's feeling (shared by a vast number of
Americans) that September 11 marked a dramatic upheaval in the
country—the world has been turned "upside down," nothing
looks the same, people feel disoriented and confused. Neil's
switching from one end of the machine gun to the other reflects
his efforts to recover from September 11, and in particular his
belief that the most important spiritual ideal to uphold in times
like these is a love for all humans, "friends" and "enemies" alike.
Neil's dream gave him a striking symbolic experience of this ideal,

and he said that by means of his dream he felt better able to appreciate its relevance to the post–September 11 world: "I have experienced both sides—the victim as well as the terrorist....I can understand intellectually how Osama bin Laden views the U.S. I have also prayed for him—that he will see his version of Islam as skewed and destructive. What he has begun, only he can end. Like it or not, we are all connected and responsible for each other—his fate is also our fate. Hate and oppression can only be defeated with love. I know this sounds naïve but Gandhi proved that it is possible."[14]

When Neil jumped at the machine gun and was surprised to find that suddenly no one was there, he saw this as a confirmation of his deepest spiritual convictions: "The message in this is, fear has no energy, do not be afraid to confront fear, it will drop away empty."[15] This is an ideal that Neil has always cherished, and in a time of great turmoil, when the whole world seems consumed by hatred and anger, his dream gave him a deeply felt *experience* of the powerful effectiveness of that ideal. In this regard Neil's dream displays the same capacity for creative meaning-making we have seen in the dreams of Melissa and others, and Neil commented on the fact that immediately after the person behind the machine gun vanishes his perspective shifts again: "Then, I am back outside, pounding on the tail, there is hope."[16] The experience of overcoming his fear within the plane is followed by his becoming an active part of the efforts to help the victims, side by side with the rescue workers whose heroism had so moved and inspired him.

As usual, there are undoubtedly further dimensions of meaning to Neil's dream. The very first part of the dream, with its emphasis on the "belly" of the plane being torn during the crash, may be a reference to issues relating to Neil's health or to the health of someone close to him. The whole plane crash scenario could also have additional significance in relation to his feelings about his career, his family, plans for the future, and so on. Freud once said, "There is at least one spot in every dream at which it is unplumbable—a navel, as it were, that is its point of contact with the unknown."[17] I would rephrase Freud's famous dictum to say that *every* spot in a dream is unplumbable and ultimately unknowable; every dream element shades off into obscure, unbounded realms of possible meaning, eluding all attempts at strict definition or categorization. This is why the practice of dream interpretation requires the ability to discern those meanings that are most important and relevant to the dreamer's life, while at the same time honestly acknowledging the possibility of *other* dimensions of meaning. As a practical matter, I suggest that caregivers not worry excessively about all the possible meanings they are *not* discovering. If something important has been missed or ignored in the interpretation of a particular dream, other dreams in the future will likely return to that theme, probably in a more insistent fashion.

The earth-shaking impact of the terrorist attack, and its core image of the planes crashing into the WTC towers, is vividly expressed in the dream of "Lynn," a fifty-four-year-old woman in Arizona who was the wife of an Army officer for more than twenty years. In the weeks following September 11, Lynn wrestled with a complex array of feelings about the terrorist attack and the country's reaction to it. She had this dream on October 11, exactly one month after the attack:

I am in this large room that appears to be on the top of the earth—I can see the slope of the earth and vast sections of sky. The few fir trees in the distance look like miniatures. There are no other buildings. It is almost as if I am inside and outside at the same time because I can see the out of doors so clearly. One wall of the room is either open or made of glass. It is night—the sky is dark. The stars and the clouds seem to be rushing by. But I know that it is really the earth that is hurling through space because the constellations of stars are changing rapidly and they are ones I've never seen before. The room has very few furnishings. There is a big screen television on the wall opposite the outdoors and I am standing near a phone. There may be another person at the far end of the room but we don't really interact. Showing on the television is the same scene that I see outside. The commentators are all gone from the studio and the feed from one camera is all that is on. I recall that earlier—it was light out-side—the television reported and showed three or five or more (it's pos-sible that the picture could not capture the extent of what was going on) airplanes in a row with their noses pointed into the earth. The "bad guys" had figured out a way to push the earth off course. The planes had revved up their engines and they were trying to push the earth out of its orbit. And, indeed, it worked—the earth is now hurling through outer space. I am on the phone trying to reach my family. We had been talk-ing before but now the phone doesn't work and I can't get through to them. Instead, the phone is showing the same scene as is on t.v. and as I see out the window. I am terrified. I know it is the end of the world.[18]

Lynn said she awoke from this dream at about 3 a.m., utterly terrified and unable to get back to sleep: "It is not until the sun comes up that the feelings of terror completely go away. I don't recall ever having had such a dream before."[19]

As with Neil's dream, Lynn's involves several highly unusual images and perspectives. Right from the beginning of the dream, when she saw the strange stars and clouds rushing by, "I knew something was grossly wrong."[20] The same incredible scene appears on the television, and then somehow on the telephone, too. The television commentators have given up and left the stu-dio, as they are evidently just as dumbstruck as Lynn. Everyone's rapt attention is focused on this apocalyptic image of the Earth "hurling through space," forced out of its orbit by "bad guys" using commercial airplanes as weapons. Lynn said the bad guys "were like the pictures of the men responsible for 9/11, or, at least, the television report seems to think the same group responsible."[21] Her difficulties in communicating with various members of her family parallels a similar theme in many other September 11-related dreams, in which people are desperately trying to protect family members from danger (such as Ann in chapter 3, and Beth's dream later). In this regard, I would take Lynn's dream as a kind of allegory for the effects of the terrorist attack on the American psyche: The world has been violently jolted out of place, we're all terrified by these airplane-flying bad guys, and we have no idea where we're going or what the future holds.

Lynn was deeply affected both by September 11 and by the U.S. bombing campaign in Afghanistan. "I had rather intense grief with periods of crying interspersed with normal but somewhat subdued interest in daily activities. I stopped watching television."[22] One of her sons was in the Navy, stationed in the Washington, D.C., area, so she felt great concern for him, and when she talked with her former husband about the terrorist attack she realized that "we have very different takes on it. He thinks we should take action and I'm just sad."[23] All of these distressing feelings were woven into Lynn's memories of living in foreign military bases, surrounded by people hostile to her and her country. Just like Melissa in chapter 1, whose dream of being in the WTC reminded her of her painful experiences in Saudi Arabia a decade earlier and her sense now of being an "outsider" among her fellow Americans, Lynn's dream reflects a similar kind of "outsider" perspective as she watches the panicked reaction to September 11. It makes her remember the psychological coping abilities she had developed to deal with the constant danger of terrorist attack:

> I am used to being in a community where people are on high alert, where an act of terrorism may be just around the corner, where cars are searched before entering a military post, where you have to show identification before you can go here or there, where people are in military gear going to the field in convoys of tanks and

trucks or undergoing biological warfare training, etc. I have lived overseas near military bases for seven years, first in Germany during the Vietnam years when terrorist attacks on American military posts were not uncommon and then around the Gulf War when the threat of terrorism increased once again. So the reality of terroris[m] toward Americans is not new to me.[24]

For Lynn, September 11 had the effect of bringing the whole country to a level of anxious vigilance that she had long ago been forced to experience. This dream really stood out for her because of its apocalyptic imagery ("I've never had a dream where I thought the world was ending"[25]) and its extreme and long-lasting sense of fear, and like the other nightmares we have discussed it expressed both the depths of her suffering and the resilience of her coping abilities. "The old world has been destroyed": That is the basic message of the dream, and a major part of its emotional impact on Lynn has involved the stimulation of renewed reflection on the strengths she drew on during comparably threatening times from the past to deal with the new and incredibly frightening global situation following September 11. How can she, and the rest of us, figure out a way to survive on a planet seemingly spinning out of control? In part, by reviving the defensive skills she learned many years ago, skills that enabled her to live and raise a family despite the continual threat of violence and death posed by an extremely hostile external environment.

Crashing into the Dominican College Area

The last airplane dream I would like to discuss is one of my own, which came the night of September 26:

I'm on a plane flight with Middle Eastern terrorists. We're flying low over San Rafael, about to crash in the Dominican College area. As the plane

81

swoops down I jump out a window and luckily land safely. I run to a crowded swimming pool and yell, "Get out now!" Many people don't believe me, but some do. Then the plane comes, and my son and I run for the shelter as the big plane slowly falls into the pool. We're under some rubble, but I think we're OK. We'll have to tap signals through the rubble, so rescue workers can find us. We're next to a big oak tree. The terrorists are all out, and they agree with each other that money is not their goal.

I had already experienced several dreams of the "More attack?" variety since September 11, but they had all been fairly oblique in their reference to the actual events of that day. For example, I had dreams of threatening wolves, bees, and criminals, and other dreams of losing things and being in danger. I could definitely see the influence of the terrorist attack in these dreams, but nothing more clearly defined than that. The September 26 dream, however, presented the first direct and explicit portrayal of the attack's emotional impact on me. I grew up in the Dominican College area of San Rafael, and have many happy memories of playing on the school's spacious campus. In my dream the impending plane crash is aimed directly at this cherished setting from my childhood, threatening something very special in my personal history. This echoes the "close to home" theme we discussed in chapter 3, and gives the first really striking expression of my emotional reaction to the terrorist attack.

Like the post–September 11 dreams of many, many other people, my dream places me in the position of the doomed passengers who were actually on board those four hijacked airplanes. I had read the news reports of the numerous cellular telephone calls made by the passengers to their loved ones in the final frantic moments before their planes crashed, and I couldn't help imagining the horror of what it must have been like to be in their place. My dream puts me *right there*: I feel almost physically ill as the plane careens wildly toward the ground, and the general sensation of powerlessness and vulnerability as we fell was intensely disturbing.[26]

However, I had a kind of "magical" power to jump out of the plane without hurting myself. I take that as a sign that my coping abilities were not completely overwhelmed by my fears; unlike those people on the planes, I had the ability to change my situation. Like Melissa in chapter 1, who runs through the World Trade Center trying to warn people of the imminent disaster, I run to a group of people and tell them to flee immediately; and like Melissa, I am ultimately unsuccessful, for the plane crashes right into the pool, and my son (my youngest child, three-and-a-half years old at the time of the dream) and I are caught in the rubble. Now my identification with the victims of September 11 shifts to the people caught in the ruins of the WTC towers, trying to signal for help from the rescue workers. Although my son and I do not seem to be physically harmed, we are still in danger, and this feeling is intensified when I hear the terrorists say they are not seeking money—they are motivated by much stronger and more dangerous passions than mere greed. Does that mean more terrorist attacks are inevitable?

Strangely, I can see through the rubble a big oak tree standing right near us, somehow unaffected by the plane crash and the resulting destruction, and I feel a small sense of hope. That's where the dream ends, and when I woke up my first association to the oak tree image was the children's book, *The Boy Who Dreamed of an Acorn*, which I had read to my youngest son at his preschool the previous day.[27] In the book a Native American boy goes on a vision quest and, to his disappointment, dreams not of a mighty eagle or powerful bear, but of a small acorn. But as the boy matures, and as the acorn grows into a tall, majestic oak tree, he comes to appreciate how the oak tree provides for the safety and well-being of a whole community of living creatures. My dream seemed to draw upon the narrative and imagery of this children's book as another way of reaffirming the fact that amidst all the death, destruction, horror, and fear in my country at that moment, I could still rely on the elemental forces of life to remain strong and standing.

I had plans to take a research trip to Boston in October, but after September 11 I cancelled them. Partly I did not want to leave home and create more upheaval for my wife and children, and partly I just didn't fancy the idea of stepping on an airplane quite yet. In mid-November I went ahead with a plane trip to an academic conference, and everything was fine—there were no security breaches, and I didn't have a panic attack. But I had the definite feeling that something had changed, and I would always have this uneasy sense of danger when flying on airplanes. In that, I suspect I am not alone.

Beyond serving as a final illustration of the plane crash theme, I offer these personal reflections as a way of encouraging caregivers to pay close attention to their own dreams. Your dreams can be a powerful source of empathetic insight into the emotional worlds of the people you are trying to help, and your dreams can also be a means of reflecting on the psychological damage you yourself may have suffered in a recent crisis or disaster. You may be surprised at what you discover when you turn your caregiving gaze inward toward your own dreaming experiences.

Essential Bibliography

Bulkeley, Kelly. 1995. *Spiritual Dreaming: A Cross-Cultural and Historical Journey*. Mahwah: Paulist Press.

———. 1999a. *Visions of the Night: Dreams, Religion, and Psychology*. Ed. R. Van de Castle, SUNY Series in Dream Studies. Albany: State University of New York Press.

Cassler, Leigh, & Shonto Begay. 1994. *The Boy Who Dreamed of an Acorn*. New York: Philomel.

Franzen, Jonathan. 2001. *New Yorker*, 9/24.

Freud, Sigmund. 1965. *The Interpretation of Dreams*. Trans. J. Strachey. New York: Avon Books.

Gregor, Thomas. 1983. Dark Dreams About the White Man. *Natural History* 92 (1):8–14.

Hobson, J. Allan. 1988. *The Dreaming Brain*. New York: Basic Books.

Irwin, Lee. 1994. *The Dream Seekers: Native American Visionary Traditions of the Great Plains*. Norman: University of Oklahoma Press.

Lincoln, Jackson Stewart. 1935. *The Dream in Primitive Cultures*. London: University of London Press.

McPhee, Charles Lambert. 2002. *Ask the Dream Doctor*. New York: Random House.

Schneider, D. M. & Lauriston Sharp. 1969. *The Dream Life of a Primitive People: The Dreams of the Yir Yoront of Australia*. Washington, D.C.: American Anthropological Association.

Tedlock, Barbara. 2001. The New Anthropology of Dreaming. In *Dreams: A Reader on the Religious, Cultural, and Psychological Dimensions of Dreaming*, ed. K. Bulkeley. New York: Palgrave.

———, ed. 1987. *Dreaming: Anthropological and Psychological Interpretations*. New York: Cambridge University Press.

Tonkinson, Robert. 1970. Aboriginal Dream-Spirit Beliefs in a Contact Situation: Jigalong, Western Australia. In *Australian Aboriginal Anthropology*, ed. R. M. Berndt. Sydney: University of Western Australia Press.

Wallace, Anthony F. C. 1958. Dreams and Wishes of the Soul: A Type of Psychoanalytic Theory Among the Seventeenth Century Iroquois. *American Anthropologist* 60:234–48.

Notes

1. Tonkinson 1970, 289. See also Schneider & Sharp 1969.
2. See, for example, Tedlock 2001, 1987; Wallace 1958; Lincoln 1935; Irwin 1994.

3. Gregor 1983, 10.
4. Gregor 1983, 12.
5. See Bulkeley 1995, chap. 6.
6. It is also not yet known if the perpetrators intentionally chose the date of September 11 (9/11) because of its symbolic association with the 911 of the U.S. emergency telephone system. My guess is that the terrorists did not intend it; they may have been clever, but they were not *that* clever. Nevertheless, many Americans have commented on the association, and I expect it will become an oft-used element in future dreams about the disaster.
7. McPhee 2002, 7–14.
8. Franzen 2001, 29.
9. I speculate that falling dreams reflect the deep roots of our being in the fundamental physics of nature. All life must struggle against the eternal pull of gravity; all animate existence represents a temporary victory over that downward pull—hence the primal joyfulness of most flying dreams and the overwhelming terror of most falling dreams.
10. Personal communication, 10/15/01.
11. Personal communications, 10/15/01 and 10/24/01.
12. For the most influential statement of this point of view, see Hobson 1988. For my critique of Hobson's ideas, see Bulkeley 1999a.
13. Personal communication, 10/24/01.
14. Personal communication, 10/24/01.
15. Personal communication, 10/17/01.
16. Personal communication, 10/17/01.
17. Freud 1965, 143, n. 2.
18. Personal communication, 11/28/01.
19. Personal communication, 11/28/01.
20. Personal communication, 11/30/01.
21. Personal communication, 11/30/01.

22. Personal communication, 11/30/01.
23. Personal communication, 11/30/01.
24. Personal communication, 11/30/01.
25. Personal communication, 11/30/01.
26. I awoke from the dream around 4 A.M., which for me is usually a signal of an especially intense dream; most of the dreams I remember and record in my journal come right before I wake up in the morning, so I always take note when I wake up in the middle of the night with a really vivid dream in mind.
27. Cassler & Begay 1994.

5. Disease

Anthrax Anxiety

The various threats we have discussed so far—crashing airplanes, terrorist attacks, warfare, domestic violence, and so on—all represent dangers we can see and perceive with our unaided eyes. The fact that we can use our visual perception abilities in such situations provides us with important adaptive advantages.[1] But what do we do when we face a threat we cannot see? Throughout our history as a species, humans have faced dangers that cannot be perceived by ordinary vision, invisible dangers that seem to come out of nowhere to wipe out whole populations, killing in a frighteningly rapid and mercilessly indiscriminate fashion. I am speaking, of course, of *germs*. Human existence is, from this perspective, a never-ending battle against the vast legions of micro-organisms relentlessly trying to consume us. We live in a world awash in germs; germs are in the food we eat, the water we drink, the air we breathe. They are everywhere around us, and billions of them dwell within each of our bodies.

To defend ourselves against these hungry, omnipresent, but visually imperceptible organisms, humans have developed over the course of evolutionary history a highly sophisticated immune system that keeps the germs at bay and allows us to live a relatively healthy, disease-free life. Our immune system possesses a primal kind of intelligence—it can "remember" its encounters with different germs and prepare itself to respond more effectively in future encounters with those same infectious agents.[2]

This deep biological intelligence compensates to a large degree for our lack of visual abilities in dealing with micro-organismic threats. However, new germs are evolving all the time, so the battle never ends, and the anxious sense of danger always remains. Even with the spectacular gains made by medical science since the invention of the microscope, humans continue to feel a profound and intensely visceral fear of disease in all its forms. The terrible plagues that swept through Europe in the Middle Ages, the devastating illnesses brought by white settlers to the indigenous people of the Americas (recall the Mehinaku dream of a plane carrying smallpox in chapter 4), the relentless outbreaks of typhus, cholera, and smallpox in the early decades of the twentieth century, the worldwide AIDS epidemic today—these and countless other micro-organismic assaults we humans have experienced through our history have left within us a deeply ingrained terror of infectious diseases, a terror that reflects the all-too-accurate recognition that such diseases pose one of the greatest threats not only to our individual survival but to the survival of our species.

Recognizing and appreciating the instinctual power of this fear of disease makes it easier to understand the panicked reaction of many Americans to the murderous use of the biological weapon anthrax in the weeks following September 11. Coming so soon after that day's unprecedented horrors, the discovery that several people had been killed and scores sickened by anthrax-tainted letters struck the nation with devastating emotional force. The shocking realization that we were vulnerable to yet *another* form of sneak attack (whether from inside or outside the country, no one knew) intensified the country's anxiety to a level few of us had ever experienced before. And worst of all, this new danger came from an especially malevolent direction—*humans using germs as weapons against other humans.* The malicious threat from anthrax was like no other assault the country had ever experienced, and as the government and medical establishment scrambled to respond it became clear how completely vulnerable we are to more such attacks in the future. Perhaps even more than what happened on September 11, the anthrax letters may be a prophetic sign of future terrorist attacks to come.

In this chapter I discuss a set of dreams involving anthrax, biological warfare, and disease. In the course of this discussion we cover several themes of special relevance to caregiving practice. One theme is the emotional impact of a second trauma soon following a first one. The psychological effects of the anthrax letters following September 11 can, in this regard, be compared to the effects of, say, a death in the family following a divorce, or a house fire following a sexual assault, or a car crash following a job loss. Special caregiving efforts must be made for people who have suffered this kind of a "double whammy" concurrence of psychologically damaging experiences.

A second theme in the chapter is the important symbolic role that disease imagery plays in dreams. Disease often serves as a personal symbol of vulnerability, weakness, decay, and lost or threatened creative vitality. It can also serve as a collective symbol of broader dangers to the community, metaphorically connecting the individual body to the society as a whole ("the body politic") and envisioning threats to society as infectious illnesses.

And a third theme is the intriguing analogy between the nature of dreaming and the way the immune system works. Antti Revonsuo, the Finnish neuroscientist whose ideas about nightmares were discussed in chapter 3, makes the following claim for the value of seeing dreaming as a psychological elaboration on the basic biological functioning of the immune system: "Exactly as the evolved biological function of the immune system is to elicit appropriate immune responses when triggered by antigens, the evolved biological function of the dream production system is to construct appropriate threat simulations when triggered by real threats....My conclusion is that the dream production system can be seen as an ancestral defense mechanism comparable to other biological defense mechanisms whose function is to automatically elicit efficient protective responses when the appropriate cues are encountered."[3]

The same analogy is used by psychotherapist Alan Siegel in helping parents understand the nightmares of their children: "Nightmares are more often like a vaccine than a poison. A vaccination infects us with a minute dose of a disease that mobilizes our antibodies and makes us more resistant to the virulence of the disease. As distressing as nightmares can be, they offer powerful information about issues that are distressing to your child. When children share their nightmares and receive reassurance from their parents, they feel the emotional sting of the dream, but they also begin the process of strengthening their psychological defenses and facing their fears with more resilience."[4]

Thinking of the literal and metaphorical dimensions of this connection between dreaming and the immune system opens up new ways of understanding the value of dreamsharing with people who are suffering various kinds of disease. At the same time as their immune systems are struggling mightily to fight off a biological attack, these people's dreaming imaginations are struggling with just as much energy to deal with the psychological distress and spiritual anguish caused by the disease. By taking the initiative to ask disease victims about their dreams and nightmares, caregivers can help the people open themselves to a remarkably free, open, and honest flow of emotional expression. Although dreamsharing cannot by itself cure people of disease, it does have the power of enhancing their conscious awareness of both their deepest fears and their greatest remaining strengths. At times of terrible suffering and vulnerability, that kind of enhanced self-awareness can have a deeply revitalizing effect on a person's survival skills and coping abilities.

Let me turn now to a dream in which disease imagery does not reflect an actual physical illness, but rather the painful emotional dimensions of a personal and collective tragedy. The dream came from "Ruth," a twenty-seven-year-old actress from New York who was out of town at a workshop on the day of the attack and returned to the city five days later. She had the dream on October 11:

I'm in Central Park. I see this tiny hot air balloon over us—I know something is wrong. It's coming closer. Then—boom—it explodes. Lots of dust or smoke. Someone says it's Anthrax. I cover my mouth. We all run to our cars. I get into a car with this sweet old couple. They are rich and will take me to their house. In the house, I scrub my hands and blow my nose. Their house is so nice. We hear Peter Jennings on the news. He says (and at the same time we see) Osama bin Laden walking across the park with a big gun and he declares war on the U.S. We are terrified—and the gas that was released is a part of our own Immuno Deficiency (? Like part of a disease we have here that he found some strand of and used it to make the Anthrax—like a strand from the AIDS virus). How he got a strand of that—we don't know. I think: Please God, I want to live. There are so many things I want to do. Life is so precious.[5]

Ruth says she rarely has nightmares, and even after September 11 she did not remember any negative, frightening dreams of the terrorist attack, despite the fact that she was in the city that day and knew numerous people who were directly affected by the destruction of the WTC towers. This dream jumped out at Ruth because it gave her such a clear portrait of September 11-generated fear, and the dream seemed to be pointing to issues not only in her life but in broader society as well.

The dream is initially set in Central Park, the city's cherished nature preserve and center for community recreational activity. As a place of relaxation, enjoyment, and "letting down one's guard," Central Park is an apt symbol for Ruth's feeling that our most precious values and ways of living are under attack. When she sees a tiny hot air balloon suddenly explode, it reemphasizes the post–September 11 realization that what used to seem harmless is now a source of terrible danger. The dust and smoke caused by the balloon explosion recall the dust and smoke generated by the collapse of the WTC towers. Public health officials immediately recognized the smoke as a serious threat in itself, and they made repeated warnings about these airborne hazards to everyone living in the greater New York area. Ruth's dream also refers specifically to the possibility that the dust contains the biological weapon anthrax. At the time of her dream the country's anxiety about anthrax was near its peak, and particularly for people on the east coast there was a widespread fear that a simple envelope in the mail could be the deadly carrier of an invisible menace. Ruth's dream brings all these themes together—an explosive attack from the air, a terrible cloud of smoke, a fearful rumor of anthrax—in a single, utterly terrifying moment. She covers her mouth to protect herself, and flees like everyone else.

The next scene offers an imagined response to this overwhelming fear. Ruth suddenly finds herself in a car with "this sweet old couple." She said the couple had a comforting quality to them, and they made her think of an elderly man she had heard in synagogue a couple weeks earlier. People were discussing their feelings about the terrorist attacks and how God could let such things happen, and this elderly man "raised his hand and said he had lived through the Holocaust, and no offense, but he is not surprised by this death and this atrocity. It is just that we Americans have no concept of this, especially people of the younger generation. This tragedy did not shock him. It was no worse than what he witnessed."[6] The elderly man's words made a big impression on Ruth (she was raised Jewish, and in recent years she had become increasingly drawn to Jewish spiritual traditions), and she felt a similar sense in her dream from the old couple: "It's like their wisdom was protecting me, their experience and their knowledge of this kind of pain, and under their 'shelter' I was somewhat safer."[7] Their beautiful house added to this feeling, and Ruth wondered if, following the common metaphorical connection in dreams between an architectural structure like a house and the individual's sense of self, "maybe this couple is a part of me, too. If I can 'live' in this house of beauty and wisdom, I will be protected from the evil happening around me."[8]

At this point in the dream Ruth feels "somewhat safer," but not totally safe—there are still dangers outside of the house, out there in the world. Having regained some degree of emotional balance, Ruth is now able to confront those dangers and, if not defeat them, at least recognize them clearly for what they are. She sees Osama bin Laden, the prime suspect in the September 11 attacks, in Central Park itself, armed with a big gun. Ruth admits she felt this image was "cartoon-like" in portraying bin Laden vainly strutting around the park with a phallic weapon of ridiculously exaggerated size. Still, she felt terrified in the dream, and his declaration of war on the United States was all the more frightening because it seemed he had somehow tied anthrax to the AIDS virus and our immune systems.

When Ruth told me this last part of the dream I couldn't quite follow what she was describing; the narrative seemed to become tangled and disjointed. So I asked Ruth if she could say anything more about what bin Laden seemed to be doing and how it related to anthrax and our "immuno deficiency." Ruth replied that the dream was definitely a response to the current news about the anthrax attacks, and she understood it as a kind of cultural commentary on what was happening to the country: "What struck me about the 'immuno deficiency' was how I/we/Americans in general felt 'immune' to anything harming our freedom and safety, and somehow that is a deficiency as far as I see it—that Osama bin Laden somehow found a 'strand' of that—that weakness in our structure, and is using it against us."[9]

So the complex dream image of anthrax, AIDS, and Osama bin Laden acts as both a personal and a collective symbol. It expresses Ruth's personal fears for the safety and security of her own life in the aftermath of September 11, and it also expresses her sense of the terrible dangers facing everyone in the country. At the very beginning of the dream she seems to "see it coming"—she intuitively knows "something is wrong," but she can't name it, and thus she can't do anything about it. By the end of the dream she has a much clearer understanding of what exactly is threatening the country, and as we have discussed at several points in the preceding chapters, the more distinctly we can identify the dangers in our environment, the better able we are to respond effectively to them.

Ruth's final appeal to the divine—"Please God, I want to live"—is like the closing prayer of an anguished religious ritual. In these unspoken words of supplication she reaffirms her essential love of life and gives testimony to the continuing emergence of a deep spirituality within her. Even though the dream was extremely frightening and upsetting, she said those last thoughts about God were "very, very comforting....I am glad that God is present in my dream life, if not so much in waking life, yet."[10] Ruth is like many other people who regard their dreams as valuable sources of spiritual insight and revelatory guidance, and especially in times of suffering these people's dreams bring them deep consolation and reassurance.

I strongly suggest that caregivers working in a crisis situation make the effort to learn about people's spiritual beliefs as quickly as possible, because those beliefs can be powerful allies in responding to the crisis. Of course, many people do not hold any distinctly religious or spiritual views, and just as it is important to openly recognize the spiritual beliefs of those who have them, it is equally important to acknowledge and respect the integrity of people who do *not* think of the world in spiritual terms. For such people, speaking of the presence of God in dreams is unlikely to be helpful. But perhaps the language of evolutionary adaptation may be more meaningful to them, and Ruth's dream is a good illustration of this approach as well as of the spiritual approach to understanding the value of dreams. Ruth's fearful realization that Osama bin Laden has found a way to exploit our country's "immuno deficiency" can be seen as an explicit metaphorical connection between the biological and the psychological defense systems of the human organism. To think of dreaming as the operation of a kind of psychological immune system makes excellent sense in connection with the latest findings of neuroscientific research, and I believe this research supports, in a perfectly secular and "nonspiritual" fashion, the active effort of caregivers to include dream discussions in their work with the victims of unexpected disasters. A spiritual orientation does seem to flow naturally from the experience of sharing and discussing dreams (recall the New York firefighter who got "rather metaphysical" in his conversation with Gloria Sturzenacker), but it is not necessary.

What would it feel like to be infected with anthrax? What would be the first symptoms? How would we know if the germs had already gotten into our bodies and were beginning the process of destroying us? In the fall of 2001 millions of Americans anxiously asked themselves these questions, as every day the media seemed to report a new discovery of anthrax-contaminated mail somewhere in the country. Where was it safe, and where was it dangerous? For several weeks, no one knew for sure. With so many people in such an extremely heightened state of vigilance, it should not be surprising to find that a large number of them had disturbingly vivid dreams in which they imaginatively anticipated what it would be like to fall victim to a biological weapon.

"Sam" is a sixty-year-old man from New Jersey who contacted me in December to ask if I could help him understand this series of dreams:

On 9/1/01 I had a dream about two twin tall buildings falling but they were not completely built yet. In this same dream there was a bomb on a nearby bridge but it did not go off. This same dream contained much traveling to the Far East, France, a South Pacific destination and a place with mountains that gets very hot and cold.

On 10/1/01 I had another dream. From my window at home in New Jersey, I saw a huge flash of light in the direction of NYC and realized that I had to wait 3 minutes for the shock wave and then death to reach me. I presumed it was a bomb.

On 10/4/01 I had a dream that I was running very fast. I woke up and my skin felt it was burning like I had a bad sunburn and prickly heat. It really hurt. A cold shower did not cool me down. I had the fear it was either a chemical/bio attack or fallout radiation burns.

On 10/22 I had a reoccurrence of the heated skin/prickly heat feeling only in my head and neck, while in bed but before I fell asleep. I fell asleep and awoke after two hours with that burning feeling all over my body and really hurt again. This time I could not recall my dream.

On 10/31 I woke up at 4:30 AM after falling asleep in a chair. I had the same prickly heat/hot skin from the neck to the elbows only. I cannot recall the dream.[11]

When I asked Sam whether he was directly impacted by September 11, he gave a reply that stunned me: Sam had worked for ten years in the WTC, and for the last five at Cantor Fitzgerald, the financial services company with its headquarters in the upper floors of the first WTC tower. Sam had recently been laid off by the company, and even though he was grateful for his own life (about losing his job he said, "Thank God!...or I would surely be dead now"[12]), he felt the incredible sorrow of personally knowing hundreds and hundreds of the people who died in the terrorist attack.

I will discuss his first dream later, in chapter 9. For now, I would like to focus on the strange skin sensations that Sam experiences both inside and outside his dreams. He said he had never felt such skin pain before, and even now his doctor said Sam was in fine health.[13] But Sam knew the burning sensations were tied to his dream of October 1, which he felt was like "the result of radioactivity of a chemical/biological attack. My home is about 35 miles from NYC and would be on the outer rim of such an explosion and would take some time before I would feel the shock and heat wave, just as I felt in the dream."[14] Like many of the dreams we have considered, this one presents an imagined anticipation of a danger in the dreamer's immediate environment. Sam's dream gives him a "preview" of what might be coming, and the intensity of his concern is evidently so great that it evokes a strong and lasting physiological reaction—the burning feelings on his skin. This kind of psychosomatic experience is fairly common among people who have just suffered a terrible emotional blow, and it indicates the extreme defensive measures they feel compelled to take to protect themselves against future attacks. Sam said, "What frightened me most was the onset of the sunburn/prickly heat sensation while I was totally awake and then continuing and escalating while asleep."[15] The strength and persistence of this distressing skin sensation had the psychological effect of keeping Sam acutely aware of the dangers of living so close to a potential target of future terrorist attacks. His dream of October 1 set in motion a powerful survival response system using both psychological and physiological processes in the battle against life-threatening dangers.

Dreaming and the Body

In this book I have been presenting an approach centered on the principle of always respecting the dreamer's own sense of what his or her dream means. My approach draws in large measure from what I have learned over the years from three people: Montague Ullman, Jeremy Taylor, and Robbie Bosnak. The methods and techniques of these three men are quite different from each other, as are their personality styles. However, all three adhere to that central principle of dreamwork *(Always respect the dreamer)*, and all three regard dreaming as a powerful means of personal and collective transformation. In addition to their consensus on these core beliefs, each of them has promoted distinctive ideas and practices that have strongly influenced my way of working with dreams. Ullman's great contribution has been to reformulate Freudian dream theory from the inside (Ullman is a practicing psychoanalyst) and open up the potential benefits of dreamsharing to people outside the context of professional therapy. Working in both the United States and Sweden, Ullman has been a pioneer in promoting dreamsharing as a basic resource for community mental health. Taylor's lifework has been teaching practical dreamwork in churches, schools, and community centers, using methods that combine Jungian psychology with Unitarian Universalist spirituality. His emphasis on the role of personal projections in group dreamsharing (the "If it were my dream" method also advocated by Ullman) has provided a welcome alternative to the rigid, dictatorial interpretations of traditional psychoanalysis. Bosnak, a practicing Jungian analyst, has written with rare eloquence about the autonomous *realness* of dream characters and settings, and he has developed a way of working with dreams that revolves around the fundamentally somatic qualities of dreaming experience. In the context of our discussion of dreams and disease, Bosnak's work has a direct caregiving relevance that is worth our further attention.

The most formative experience I had with Bosnak came in 1991, when I attended a dream studies conference that he organized called "Dreaming in Russia." Held at a small meeting center outside Moscow, this gathering was billed as the first major encounter among American, European, and Soviet dream researchers. By the strangest of fortunes those of us flying from the United States arrived in Moscow on the afternoon of Monday, August 19, 1991—one of the last planes allowed to land before the airport was closed by Red Army troops as part of the fateful military coup against Mikhail Gorbachev and his reform-minded Soviet government. Everyone who had arrived for the conference was shocked and frightened, of course, and the next three days were a crazed blur of inscrutable pronouncements from the coup leaders, vain attempts to telephone home, and international, multicultural dreamsharing. The incredible political and social chaos around us provided an almost otherworldly context in which to discuss our thoughts and feelings about dreams. I have written elsewhere about my own experiences during the "Dreaming in Russia" conference;[16] here I want to share the experiences of Michael Dupre, my roommate in the conference center dormitory, who wrote a lyrical article for the journal *Dreaming* titled "Russia. Dreaming. Liberation."[17]

Michael was in his thirties, a New Yorker, and, for the previous two years, a person living with the knowledge that he had AIDS. AIDS was a disease that literally reached into Michael's guts, causing him serious gastro-intestinal problems that he knew could take a fatal turn at any moment: "Having AIDS certainly has put me into contact with my own mortality. Of course, living with this knowledge is at the very least a two-edged sword. People with AIDS are constantly living 'under the sword,' knowing it could drop at any moment. Another edge is the realization of the importance of doing and living what brings out the passion in your soul. That is what brought me to this conference of dreams. I've cultivated my dreams like a garden, ever so slowly, since about the age of four."[18]

After our plane landed, Michael and the rest of us made the bus trip from the airport to the conference center (seeing dozens of tanks rumbling along the freeway in the other direction, toward Moscow). Once we got ourselves settled in our rooms, the conference proceeded more or less as scheduled. But all the while we

100

were acutely aware that the whole world around us seemed to be going crazy. Gorbachev was missing, reportedly "ill" and removed for his health to an undisclosed location; the television news showed intimidating images of Red Army troops, tanks, and armored personnel carriers positioned throughout the city to "preserve public safety," while rumors flew that a resistance movement was building and a violent confrontation possible at any time. Being cut off from any communication with the outside world, everyone at the conference naturally felt a high degree of anxiety. But for Michael, as for many of the rest of us, there was at the same time a strange pleasure in the radical shift of perception and orientation toward the world. Despite his fears, "the release from my own day-to-day egocentrism into the more global concern remained in the forefront. So indescribably refreshing. Parched lips and water from the Well."[19]

In that expanded psychosocial context, Michael had a dream:

I dream that I'm in my room at the conference center. Suddenly, I notice there are a number of bugs, of different shapes and sizes on the wall. The scariest ones are these two big knob-shaped black bugs. I think I cannot live with them, and I go to get a shoe to smash them. I also think how disgusting that's going to be. I turn around, and they've crawled down the wall behind the storage space, making it very difficult if not impossible to be rid of them.[20]

When Michael shared this dream with the rest of us (his dream was the first one discussed in a full group setting), it elicited a variety of strong reactions all revolving around the many symbolic dimensions of the image of *bugs*. Bugs as insects, bothersome and potentially dangerous. Bugs as disease, germs infecting our bodies and making us ill. Bugs as threats to travelers in foreign countries, infesting the food, water, and air. "Being bugged" as being annoyed or irritated, perhaps in connection with being forced to live in close quarters with a group of strangers. "Being bugged" as being under surveillance by spies and secret police, being watched, observed, judged. This last theme felt especially strong for Michael: "The collective anxiety and fear and paranoia had entered my psyche as if by osmosis. I was not immune. Not immune."[21]

Three days after we arrived in Russia, the coup attempt abruptly ended. There had been some violence in Moscow, and several protestors were killed. But the "bad guys" had evidently lost, and spontaneous celebrations filled the streets, although no one really knew what the "good guys" (led by Moscow's mayor Boris Yeltsin) were going to do after the shockingly swift collapse of the entire Soviet government. The intense fear we experienced during the previous three days all but evaporated, though the confusion and uncertainty were still just as strong, and now an extra element of sorrow had emerged in recognition of the tragic death of the three protestors. A funeral procession through Moscow was quickly organized to commemorate their sacrifice, and Michael made a point of traveling into the city to join in that public ritual of mourning, where he was "hoping to release some of my own personal grief over the loss of thirty-some dear friends and acquaintances over the last half dozen years."[22]

A day later, Michael had a more serendipitous experience of ritualized mourning when he came with the conference group on a sightseeing trip to the spectacular Russian Orthodox monastery at Zagorsk. He found himself strangely moved as he watched the faithful praying in the sanctuaries, lighting candles before lovingly painted icons, and venerating the remains of cherished saints.

All of these elements came together in Michael's next dream, which he titled "Facing Death" and which he shared in a small group setting with Bosnak as the leader. I want to share this piece of dreamwork because it illustrates so well Bosnak's focus on the bodily sensations that emerge in and through our dreaming experience. Here is Michael's dream:

I am in the chapel at Zagorsk. After some contemplation, I join the short line of pilgrims to participate in a ritual. Each individual, one at a time, walks up to the sarcophagus and bestows three kisses: at the feet, the chest, and the head. After each kiss the penitent performs the Eastern orthodox sign of the cross: the left hand touches the forehead, below the heart, the left shoulder and then the right. When it is my turn, I kiss the glass top three times, but with each kiss, I raise my lips a little higher, so by the time I come to where the head is, I'm actually kissing air. In addition, for fear of fumbling, I make the Roman sign of the cross, using my right hand to touch my head, my sternum, my left and then my right shoulder. After the last kiss, my dream no longer replays what occurred. I turn and join a small party of people. We are still in the chapel, but there is an atmosphere of socializing. We are eating sandwiches with chunks of meat inside. I realize these are the discarded parts of a woman diagnosed with multiple-personality disorder. We are the last step in her process of becoming more whole. Then I am suddenly overcome by revulsion. I think: "This is cannibalism!" I start feeling nauseous, like I'm going to throw up. I feel so sick that mentally I jump back into rationalization to justify what it is we're doing. We are helping her to rid her life of unwanted parts, assimilate what needs to be assimilated. But then the feeling of absolute disgust returns.[23]

Michael acknowledged that the image of the woman with multiple-personality disorder (MPD) was at one level a reference to the "gossipy outrage floating about the conference" regarding the moral proprieties of a presenter's acknowledgment that he had recently married a woman with MPD who had initially come to him for clinical treatment. But for Michael there were deeper levels to the dream than that, which emerged in the following discussion with Robbie Bosnak (Michael's interpretive comments from the article are rendered in italics):

R: "So how do you feel about eating these cannibal sandwiches?"

M: "*I feel disgusted and disgusting.*"

R: "Can you place those feelings in your body?"

M: "Yes, in the pit of my stomach. I feel very nauseous. The more I think of it, the sicker I feel. I'm afraid I might vomit."

This was a cue to move to another image, at least temporarily:

R: "How do you feel looking at the saint's remains?"

M: "I feel solemnity. I feel a vague reverence."

R: "In your body?"

M: "I don't feel anything. Well, I feel a stillness overall. My body and mind are calm and clear."

The two poles are presenting themselves more vividly.

R: "So, what about those cannibal sandwiches?"

M: "As a cannibal sandwich, I know I'm dead meat. Putrification is taking hold. I know I will soon be rotting in someone's stomach. As the eater of the sandwich, my stomach is churning. I'm afraid of getting very sick."

R: "What is it like to participate in the kissing ritual?"

M: "It's strange and strangely familiar."

R: "Where in your body is all of this?"

M: "I almost feel bodyless."

R: "What do you mean?"

M: "My whole body feels light."

R: "And that final kiss, when your lips do not touch the glass?"

M: "I feel like I'm kissing the invisible."

A spontaneous metaphor on the part of the dreamer suggests stirrings from the unconscious.

R: "What is it like to kiss the invisible?"

M: "I feel light. I feel lightness. I feel elevated. I feel at peace."

R: "What about when you go back to the sandwich party? Do you still experience nausea?"

M: "No, I've carried the sensation of lightness with me."

R: "Where are you carrying it?"

M: "In the pit of my stomach. There's a circle of light."

Ah ha, the paradox. The grotesque and the sublime finding resolution in the pit of the stomach. A circle of light in the part of my body where AIDS has caused me the most physical suffering and where I have carried my worst fears of the disease as well. Each pole of the paradox represents different faces of death. Indeed, in each instance I am "facing" death: the eating and the kissing.[24]

Michael's dream brings together death and life, horror and hope, darkness and lightness, matter and spirit. In this creative tension of opposites he finds new emotional resources for dealing with his personal struggles and with the chaotic world around him.

This account from Michael's experiences in Russia gives a good picture of Bosnak's basic approach to dreams. His questions are intended to guide Michael to focus his awareness on the physical dimensions of his dream's images, to the point where Michael can *feel* each image somewhere in his body. Once Michael has developed this embodied awareness of the various dream images, Bosnak leads him to concentrate on the point of greatest tension and opposition in the dream, and out of that tension emerges a burst of new energy, insight, and symbolic understanding. Following Jung, Bosnak likens this to the alchemical process of combining opposing elements to produce a new and greater whole, and in Michael's case the conflict in his dream between the disgust in his stomach and the lightness of his kiss finds a sudden symbolic resolution in the appearance of a circle of light in his stomach.

This body-centered method of dreamwork does not work for everyone (no method does), but I would encourage caregivers to follow Bosnak's lead and ask questions about the bodily sensations that accompany dream images (particularly strong or unusual images). If the questions don't lead anywhere, then leave it be, and try something else. But oftentimes these questions *will* lead somewhere. Particularly for people living in a society that sharply distinguishes the mind from the body, dreams can reveal the subtle but powerful influence of bodily sensations on everything we do.[25] As the dreams of disease discussed in this chapter suggest, dreaming is the psychological expression of deep life processes that operate at every level of our being, from the microscopic workings of our immune system to the cosmic sweep of our spiritual reflections.

Personal Projections

I want to offer one last dream story related to the theme of dreaming and disease, a dream that "Kate," a twenty-seven-year-old woman living in Ohio, told me a couple months after September 11. One of the issues I want to highlight in relation to Kate's experience is the tricky role of persona projections in dream interpretation, and for that reason I invite readers to pay close attention to their own feelings, ideas, and associations as they arise while reading this dream:

I can't remember the whole dream but what I do remember is this I'm on Main Street in my hometown and I'm in the front seat of a good friend's car. I feel very sick, my nose burns. I ask her to stop the car and when she does I get out and I'm sort of hunched over, I bring my arms to my face and blood pours out of my nose into my hands, I know I have been exposed to anthrax. I can't remember who or where but I think it is a terrorist who then tells me it is my own fault for being so stupid and going to the movies on that particular night and I was warned. I was terrified and felt helpless, it was one of those dreams you wake up from and it takes you a second to realize it was a dream.[26]

Kate says "it was one of those dreams"—that's right, most dreams are not like this, most dreams are pretty mundane, emotionally mild affairs with no special impact on waking awareness. Indeed, as the past several decades of sleep laboratory research have demonstrated, we humans tend to forget the vast majority of our dreaming experiences. Our REM-stimulated brains are generating dreams all through the night, every night of our lives, yet we remember at most only one or two dreams a night, and most people remember far fewer than that. It seems that none of us ever recalls more than a tiny fraction of our total dreaming experience.[27] To put it bluntly, most dreams are eminently forgettable. They make no special demands on our waking attention, and whatever functions they are serving evidently do not require conscious awareness to proceed. But things are different when we have what Kate calls "one of those dreams," a dream that hits us with an extremely powerful *realism* that momentarily crosses over from dreaming into waking awareness ("It takes you a second to realize it was a dream"). We have already discussed a number of dreams with this kind of carryover effect, and by now I hope readers have come to recognize this element as one major sign that a dream is giving a uniquely revelatory insight into the dreamer's predominant emotional concerns in waking life.

For Kate, the first clue to understanding her dream was the setting, "Main Street in my hometown." Kate said her family had owned businesses along this street throughout her life, so it was very much a physical center of the home world in which she grew up. She noted that in the dream she and her friend were driving at the opposite end of the street from the location of her family's current business, near the place where she had her first job. This made her think the dream might be representing a "search for independence"—moving away from the comfortable sphere of her family home and journeying in new directions in life. But in the dream Kate's move away from home leads her into terrible danger. She is suddenly afflicted with a strange burning pain in her nose; blood flows into her hands, and she realizes she has been infected by anthrax.

When I asked Kate if she could say anything more about this part of the dream, she replied that regarding "the pain and bleeding from my nose as far as I know they are not typical symptoms in waking life, but in my dream I knew them to be symptoms, and I remember feeling like if this is already happening I don't have long. I also had a feeling of responsibility, like in some way it was my own fault."[28]

When I heard this from Kate, several ideas immediately came to my mind. First, I thought of the common symbolic association in many cultures between flowing blood, menstruation, and female creativity.[29] For example, an elder of the Sioux people of North America told a researcher: "When a woman is having her time, her blood is flowing, and this blood is full of mysterious powers that are related to child bearing. At this time she is particularly powerful. To bring a child into the world is the most powerful thing in creation. A man's power is nothing compared to this and he can do nothing compared to it. We respect that power."

I also thought of something I once read by anthropologist Gil Herdt on the Sambia people of New Guinea. Herdt has done extensive fieldwork studying the rituals of male initiation among the Sambia, which aim to sever, dramatically and decisively, a boy's ties to his mother and recreate his identity in the form of a pure male warrior. One of the Sambia men's most distinctive practices is the ceremonial use of stiff blades of grass to poke up their noses until they are bleeding freely. This nose-bleeding practice is obviously a very painful experience, and it is forced on young boys when they are initiated into manhood, but when they get older many Sambia men frequently make their own noses bleed as a voluntary ritual reaffirmation of their virility and warrior identity. What came back to my mind about Herdt's research on the Sambia was this sentence: "Boys symbolically learn in ritual that this blood [from the nose-bleeding] is the contaminated femaleness of boys—which represents the womb, nurturance, softness, and curses, an essence of femaleness that cannot become an essence of maleness."[30]

And right after that, I found myself thinking of Sigmund Freud and his intimate friend Wilhelm Fliess, whose theory of the psychophysiological connection between the female genitals and the nose led to one of the most horrifying experiences of Freud's life: the two of them botched an operation on a young woman's nose, and at one point a gush of blood burst out from her nose, nearly killing her.[31]

With all these strange, far-flung ideas running through my mind, I knew that Kate's dream, whatever else it might mean, had stimulated some strong personal reactions in *me*. That is always something to watch for in working with dreams, particularly with highly memorable "big" dreams—such dreams regularly evoke surprising personal reactions in the people listening to them. Freud called these feelings "transference," and Jung referred to them as "projections." These two terms highlight a crucial feature not just of dream interpretation but of all forms of human interaction: the inevitable influence of our own wishes, desires, and fears on our perception of and behavior toward other people. To acknowledge this kind of personal involvement is not necessarily a bad thing, because it signals a real connection of empathetic imagination between the dreamer and his or her listeners, and every form of caregiving depends on the establishment of such feelings of genuine interpersonal rapport. My view is that when caregivers find themselves reacting strongly to what another person has said, they may find it helpful to share their personal responses as a way of deepening the emotional honesty of the conversation—but only if the caregivers make it clear that the responses are *theirs* and do not necessarily correspond to what the other person may be feeling. The "If it were my dream" preface is the simplest way to communicate that vital principle.[32]

So, as I thought of the various symbolic associations that came up for me regarding this striking image of nose-bleeding, I wondered if any of them could help to shed light on Kate's dream. Prefacing my comments with the reminder that only the dreamer can know for sure what his or her dream means, I said that if I were a woman and had this dream I might see it as an expression of fear about how September 11 and its aftermath poses a threat to my (and, as a collective symbol, all of society's) ability to create new life, with the sudden blood flow from the nose symbolizing a kind of abnormal, pathological menstrual flow. The infection of anthrax from the male terrorist, who tells me it's "my own fault," sounded like a kind of symbolic rape, which for me echoes the hypermasculine aggression of the terrorist attacks. The familiar setting of the dream made me feel it was showing how the war is "close to home," and the detail about being at the end of the street away from the family business and close to the location of the first job brought to mind efforts to grow up and become an independent, mature person, which as a woman is often connected to having a first child.

As a final comment (after repeating my caution about these being *my* feelings and not necessarily hers), I asked Kate if there were any troubles in her relationship with the close friend she is with in the dream, the one driving the car.

Kate replied that she agreed with my reading of the dream (I felt some relief at hearing this), and in regard to my last question she said she was beginning to see that the dream had more to do with her friend than she had initially thought:

She is a very close friend but someone I have been experiencing great frustration with lately....Just to give you a little background, the troubles I'm having with my friend come down to her unwillingness to grow up and start taking responsibility for her life. A lot of her negative qualities are unfortunately also downfalls I have seen in myself which I have been very concisely trying to change. So you see, I think in my dream I am traveling down a "familiar road with her," which has negative results. I feel like it is my fault and could have been avoided. Much like in waking life I feel like traveling down her road so to speak will only bring negative results. As for the feeling of responsibility I have in my dream, I think it is telling me I do in fact have the power to control the road I choose to take.[33]

Although the dream portrayed an unforgettably frightening experience, Kate was able by the end of our conversation to recognize both the dangers facing her and the strengths she has within her to face those dangers. "When it all fell together it was very empowering. It really helped me realize my life is in my hands."[34]

Essential Bibliography

Belicki, Kathryn. 1986. Recalling Dreams: An Examination of Daily Variation and Individual Difference. In *Sleep and Dreams: A Sourcebook*, ed. J. Gackenbach. New York: Garland.

Bulkeley, Kelly. 1999a. *Visions of the Night: Dreams, Religion, and Psychology*. Ed. R. Van de Castle, SUNY Series in Dream Studies. Albany: State University of New York Press.

Damasio, Antonio. 1999. *The Feeling of What Happens: Body and Emotion in the Making of Consciousness*. San Diego: Harcourt.

Dupre, Michael. 1992. Russia. Dreaming. Liberation. *Dreaming* 2 (2):123–34.

Gay, Peter. 1988. *Freud: A Life for Our Time.* New York: W. W. Norton.

Herdt, Gilbert. 1987. *The Sambia: Ritual and Gender in New Guinea.* Fort Worth: Holt, Rinehart, and Winston.

Irwin, Lee. 2001 Sending a Voice, Seeking a Place: Visionary Traditions Among Native Women of the Plains. In *Dreams: A Reader on the Religious, Cultural, and Psychological Dimensions of Dreaming,* ed. K. Bulkeley. New York: Palgrave.

Pinker, Steven. 1997. *How the Mind Works.* New York: W. W. Norton.

Revonsuo, Antti. 2000. The Reinterpretation of Dreams: An Evolutionary Hypothesis of the Function of Dreaming. *Behavioral and Brain Sciences* 23 (6).

Taylor, Jeremy. 1983. *Dream Work.* Mahwah: Paulist Press.

———. 1992. *Where People Fly and Water Runs Uphill.* New York: Warner Books.

Ullman, Montague, & Nan Zimmerman. 1979. *Working with Dreams.* Los Angeles: Jeremy Tarcher.

Notes

1. For more on the importance of the visual perception system in the development of human intelligence see Pinker 1997, particularly chaps. 1 and 4.
2. See Revonsuo 2000, 39.
3. Revonsuo 2000, 39–40.
4. Revonsuo 2000, 91.
5. Personal communication, 10/12/01.
6. Personal communication, 10/18/01.
7. Personal communication, 10/18/01.
8. Personal communication, 10/18/01.

9. Personal communication, 10/13/01.
10. Personal communication, 10/13/01.
11. Personal communication, 12/19/01.
12. Personal communication, 12/22/01.
13. I suggested to Sam that if his strange skin sensations became debilitating in any way he should consult with a physician.
14. Personal communication, 12/21/01.
15. Personal communication, 12/21/01.
16. Bulkeley 1999a, chap. 13.
17. Dupre 1992.
18. Dupre 1992, 125.
19. Dupre 1992.
20. Dupre 1992, 125–26.
21. Dupre 1992, 126.
22. Dupre 1992. 128.
23. Dupre 1992, 131–32.
24. Dupre 1992, 131–32.
25. See Damasio 1999.
26. Personal communication, 10/30/01.
27. Belicki 1986.
28. Personal communication, 10/30/01.
29. Quoted in Irwin 2001, 99.
30. Herdt 1987, 185.
31. Gay 1988, 84.
32. See Ullman & Zimmerman 1979; Taylor 1983, 1992.
33. Personal communications, 10/30/01 and 11/15/01.
34. Personal communication, 11/15/01.

6. Bad Guys

Unconscious Racial Profiling

In my dreams a Middle Eastern looking man has suddenly appeared who keeps threatening my family. He pops out of closets or behind desks with knives or guns. What is most striking is his Middle Eastern features and how scary they are in my dream, how threatening he looks. I usually wake up right after seeing him, afraid.[1]

This report comes from "Beth," a thirty-five-year-old history graduate student and mother of two young children in Vermont, and her experience shows that people's waking reactions to a disaster do not always match the reactions of their dreaming imagination. Beth said she thought (in her waking life) that one of the saddest consequences of the terrorist attack has been the increase in violence against Arab Americans, people who had nothing to do with the attack and who abhorred its cruelty as much as anyone, yet who were being persecuted because they appeared to share the same religious, ethnic, and/or national identity as the terrorists. But to her distress, Beth admitted that in her dreams she was doing exactly what she was trying *not* to do in her waking life: "The thing that has struck me most is that my unconscious seems guilty of racial profiling—something my conscious mind resists strongly."[2] I asked her if she could describe her dream attacker in any further detail, and if she had any ideas about his purpose or motivation. She replied,

> The man who popped up several times in my dreams
> was more or less the same. Interestingly, he was beard-

less and in Western clothes—I suppose I had noted how the terrorists blended in—but I knew that he was Muslim in the dream—I guess because of dark features, or just because that was the import of the dream image. His menacing face came right out of Hollywood movies. What seemed to be motivating him was simply criminal violence, the desire to attack someone and this time it was me and my family. As I mentioned, each time I would wake up right after he appeared. The dreams during those nights were fairly fragmented, so I do not remember a larger narrative, just a sense of things being all right and then this boogie man appearing.[3]

In the days immediately following September 11, President Bush and virtually every other government official spoke out against racial profiling and prejudice against Muslims, Arabs, Middle Easterners, or anyone who simply "looked" like a terrorist. Speaking at the Islamic Center of Washington, D.C., President Bush said, "America counts millions of Muslims amongst our citizens, and Muslims make an incredibly valuable contribution to our country....And they need to be treated with respect. In our anger and emotion, our fellow Americans must treat each other with respect." As the dreams of Beth indicate, the president's moral admonitions were well justified. Just days after the attack, the frightening images of Osama bin Laden and his dark-skinned, turban-wearing, zealously religious followers had deeply imprinted themselves in the national psyche. The terror Americans felt in response to September 11 could not help but trigger intense, primal fears aimed at anyone who even remotely resembled the people responsible for the attack. This kind of knee-jerk prejudice is, of course, itself a source of terrible injustice, and that was the exact point of the comments from President Bush and the others.

But the struggle to overcome our instinctive fearfulness and preserve our ethical good sense will take more than eloquent words, more than the noble ideals and intentions of our waking selves. Among other things, it will require much greater attention to the deep emotional cross-currents revealed in our dreaming experience, and it will require a real effort to integrate those dreaming insights with our waking awareness.

As Beth's case suggests, this can be a surprisingly humbling process. Dreams are unsparingly honest in portraying the full array of our fears, foibles, and insecurities, and they force us to confront the inescapable *reality* of those parts of ourselves we do not want to admit into our waking-world sense of self. If, however, we can find a way to endure the painful realization of our own vulnerability and fearfulness (a big "if," I admit), we may find in those painful dreams a unique opportunity to expand our sense of self in unexpected new directions, bringing into conscious awareness vital energies that had never before been accessible to waking reflection. We may also find this to be a highly effective means of promoting precisely those community ideals expressed so forcefully by President Bush and the others in the days following September 11. The more that people honestly face the ego-deflating reality of their own "unconscious racial profiling," the better able they will be to make good, well-reasoned moral distinctions in their waking-life dealings with people from different backgrounds.

"Bad guy" dreams have many of the characteristics of what Carl Jung called the "shadow archetype." I regard the shadow as the key archetype of Jung's thinking because it reflects the foundational concept of his model of the mind, namely the distinction between consciousness and the unconscious. The human mind has two diametrically opposed modes of functioning, Jung said, one the "light" mode of conscious awareness, reasoning, and morality, and the other the "dark" mode of unconscious instinct, emotion, and desire. Of course, Jung was not the first person to come up with this theory of a distinction between conscious and unconscious realms of the mind. As Henri Ellenberger made clear in *The Discovery of the Unconscious*, there is a long history to the idea of psychological forces existing outside conscious awareness, a history reaching back in Western scientific thought at least to the medical investigations of Franz Mesmer in late eighteenth-century France.[4] Jung was clearly influenced by this conceptual tradition, and his psychological ideas were most directly shaped by Sigmund Freud, who for ten years was Jung's mentor, confidante, and role model. Although Jung eventually broke with Freud (for reasons that are still controversial), he always retained Freud's basic framework for approaching consciousness and the unconscious.[5] The most significant change Jung made to Freud's model was the identification of specific patterns of energy in the unconscious, patterns that had their roots not in the personal life of the individual but in the primal instincts of the human species (the "collective unconscious"). Jung personified these powerful instinctual patterns in the form of "archetypes," and in so doing he made it easier to identify their symbolic presence in dreams, myths, religion, art, and many other kinds of cultural expression.

Among all the archetypes Jung identified, the shadow plays an especially crucial role in symbolizing the fact that the mind of each individual has, in addition to a conscious sense of self, a vast realm of unconscious psychological activity. As is true with many of Jung's ideas, this one came to him in a dream. He says in his autobiography, *Memories, Dreams, Reflections*, that when he was a young man trying to decide which course of study to pursue in school, he had a dream "which both frightened and encouraged me":

It was night in some unknown place, and I was making slow and painful headway against a mighty wind. Dense fog was flying along everywhere.

117

I had my hands cupped around a tiny light which threatened to go out at any moment. Everything depended on my keeping this little light alive. Suddenly I had the feeling that something was coming up behind me. I looked back, and saw a gigantic black figure following me. But at the same moment I was conscious, in spite of my terror, that I must keep my little light going through the night and wind, regardless of all dangers.[6]

Jung saw the dream as a revelation that he must go forward in life, into the world of light, work, and responsibility—but wherever he went, a huge dark presence would always loom around him, the eerie shadows cast into the vast reaches of the unconscious by the illumination of his little light of consciousness.

In his later writings Jung spoke about the shadow more often than any other archetype, reflecting the great significance he assigned it in people's mental lives. To confront one's shadow, accept its reality no matter how "immoral" or "uncivilized" it may appear, and integrate its energy into conscious awareness—that is the essential task of human development, what Jung called *individuation*. Jung took special interest in the appearance of shadow images in nightmares, because he saw frightening dreams as painful but extremely accurate portrayals of conflict between conscious ideals and unconscious desires. When Jung worked with clients in psychotherapeutic contexts he would take nightmares as opportunities to encourage his clients to admit the existence of those desires into conscious awareness, where they could be examined, evaluated, and eventually integrated into the conscious personality. In this sense, dealing with the shadow can be regarded as the essential starting point for Jungian therapy.

Think back, if you will, to Beth's experience of being chased by the Middle Eastern bad guy. At one level her dream is an overt expression of fear about actual dangers in her waking world. Her community has suddenly been attacked, she and her loved ones may be in danger, she's not sure how to gauge the risks, and she's especially wary of people who "look" a certain way. Beth's dreams anticipate what her response would be if those waking-world dangers were actually to strike at her. However, along with this outward orientation, Beth's dreams also have an inner orientation. Her consciously stated belief about the injustice of prejudice against Middle Eastern people stands in stark symbolic opposition to her frightening dreams of being attacked by a man whose main identifying characteristic is being Middle Eastern. Following a Jungian line of thought, Beth's dreams may be understood as expressing unconscious instincts and desires that have not been sufficiently integrated into her waking consciousness. She may speak of the values of tolerance and respect, and these values may indeed represent Beth's truest ideals. But outside the light of her conscious awareness, in the shadowy regions of her unconscious mind. Beth's is terribly afraid for the well-being of her family and acutely sensitive toward people who resemble the September 11 terrorists. These feelings may be selfish, prejudiced, and irrational—but they are real, and they do not go away simply because we morally chastise ourselves for having them. Whether we like it or not, the inescapable reality of the shadow must be accepted. As Prospero says of the deformed savage Caliban at the end of *The Tempest*, "This thing of darkness I acknowledge mine."[7]

This conflict between conscious ideals and unconscious desires plays itself out not only in each individual psyche, but in the broader community as well. Jung spoke at length of the tragic role the shadow archetype plays in public matters of war, politics, and international affairs. Too often, he said, humans have projected their fears onto other people, treating them as the embodiment of the despised unconscious elements of their own selves. Projection of the shadow is, in this sense, the psychological origin for the whole long, sad history of human prejudice and persecution against people who have different colored skin, different religious beliefs, or different cultural traditions.

Jung's final years were spent in the 1950s, after the end of World War II and just at the beginning of the nuclear arms race that would consume so much energy for the next half-century and that would eventually come to threaten all life on the planet. It makes sense, then, that in discussing the social implications of the shadow Jung focused special attention on the Cold War tensions between the "good" side of Western Europe and the United States and the "evil" side of the Soviet Union. In the following passage from *Man and His Symbols* Jung laments the misguided attempts to use military or economic means alone to deal with this extremely volatile geopolitical conflict. Building bigger and bigger missiles, fighting proxy wars in third world countries, and stoking the fires of industrial development could never resolve what was ultimately a psychological conflict:

> All such attempts have proved singularly ineffective, and will do so as long as we try to convince ourselves and the world that it is only *they* (i.e., our opponents) who are wrong. It would be much more to the point for us to make a serious attempt to recognize our own shadow and its nefarious doings. If we could see our shadow (the dark side of our nature), we should be immune to any moral and mental infection and insinuation. As matters now stand, we lay ourselves open to every infection, because we are really doing practically the same thing as *they*. Only we have the additional disadvantage that we neither see nor want to understand what we ourselves are doing, under the cover of good manners.[8]

Jung's ideas about the political dimensions of the shadow dovetail remarkably well with the work of historian John Dower, whose book *War Without Mercy: Race and Power in the Pacific War* offers a frightening portrait of the violent racial prejudice that consumed both Americans and Japanese during World War II.[9]

Using examples from popular songs, political speeches, newspaper cartoons, propaganda films, and military battle plans, Dower argues that the sickening brutality of the Pacific War was fueled by the psychological effects of dehumanizing the enemy "other." If the enemy was branded as evil, inhuman, beastly, and alien, that made it not only acceptable but actually imperative to destroy him utterly, "without mercy." Dower's book is perhaps the best case study ever written on the violent political effects of two communities collectively projecting shadow elements onto each other. Dower does not go into any detail about the specific psychological mechanisms involved in the American–Japanese conflict, but what he does say is clearly congenial with Jung's basic ideas. At one point in his book Dower pauses from his discussion of the Pacific War to consider parallels with the dehumanizing rhetoric of other wars in other periods of history, and he starts with a surprising quotation:

> "Although these barbarians are not altogether mad, yet they are not far from being so....They are not, or are no longer, capable of governing themselves any more than madmen or even wild beasts and animals...." These quotations were, in fact, written in the early sixteenth century by Spaniards rationalizing the devastation of the Indian populations in the New World as a just war; [we can] substitute "Japanese" not only for the names of other races and peoples, but also for references to non-Christians, to women, to the lower classes, and to criminal elements. This is not a mere conjuror's trick. Rather, it points to the basic categories through which male-dominated Western elites have perceived and dealt with others over the centuries. Like the mark of the beast, the categories of the primitive, the child, and the mentally and emotionally deficient

enemy—which in World War II often seemed to be so specifically applicable to the Japanese, and even to entail new intellectual breakthroughs peculiar to the Japanese—were basically formulaic concepts, encoded in the Western psyche and by no means reserved for the Japanese alone.[10]

Elsewhere in the book Dower speaks of "archetypal figures" and "paradigmatic concepts," indicating his recognition of the deep unconscious roots of these psychologically and politically powerful symbols.[11] Very much like Jung, he emphasizes the adaptability of shadow projections to different times and circumstances—they are "free-floating and easily transferred from one target to another, depending on the exigencies and apprehensions of the moment. The war hates and races of World War II, that is, proved very adaptable to the cold war."[12]

I do not want to push the similarities between Jung and Dower too far, because there are real differences in their perspectives. But considered in the context of our interests, their agreement about the potentially destructive interplay of psychological and political symbolism has the effect of dramatically raising the stakes for caregiving in times of collective disaster. Jung and Dower make us realize that shadow images are activated in almost every kind of collective crisis, especially those involving war, terrorism, and political violence. The enemy is demonized, "our" side adopts a heroic pose, and the conflict is cast as a battle between good and evil. Caregiving in such situations cannot be fully effective unless it recognizes the broader social and political context in which people are trying to overcome their suffering and reorient themselves in the world. The goal should be helping people learn how to distinguish real external threats from unconscious shadow projections, thus enabling the people to respond appropriately in social and political disputes without succumbing to "unconscious racial profiling," in Beth's memorable phrase.[13]

This has become an increasingly urgent social task, as Dower himself indicates in the final pages of *War Without Mercy*. He says the last year of World War II, which of course culminated in the United States dropping atomic bombs on the Japanese cities of Hiroshima and Nagasaki (an event that has reverberated through people's nightmares for half a century), marked an unprecedented increase in the destructive potential of racial prejudice, war hates, and shadow projections of all kinds: "Holy wars were surely not new. The techniques of mobilizing and sustaining such sentiments at fever pitch had, however, advanced by quantum leaps in the twentieth century—now involving not only the sophisticated use of radio, film, and other mass media, but also a concerted mobilization and integration of the propaganda resources of the whole state apparatus. Such developments went hand in hand with breathtaking advances in the technologies of destruction, especially in air power and firepower."[14]

Dower's words, written in 1986, ring truer than ever now. We find ourselves at the beginning of the twenty-first century living in a world of horrible violence and bitter religious conflict, with each side castigating the other as evil, demonic, and inhuman. The weapons of destruction—from hijacked airplanes, biological agents, and suicide bombers to laser-guided missiles and "daisy cutter" bombs—have become astonishingly deadly, and the power of the global media to transmit emotionally captivating, ideologically driven images to vast numbers of people has never been greater. More than ever, we need to develop a self-critical understanding of our own shadow projections as an essential element in the process of responding effectively and proportionately to actual threats and dangers in the world.[15]

Nan's Dreams of Phil

We have already discussed Nan's dreams in terms of what they did *not* contain—any explicit references to her car accident. Now I want to look at what her dreams *did* contain, specifically at the most frequently appearing character: her ex-husband Phil. Her sixth dream following the accident (chapter 3) portrayed Phil as moving back into her house, with Nan helpless to stop his unwanted intrusion on her freedom and independence. In the twenty-six dreams Nan recorded during the six months after the accident, Phil appears in seven of them, far more than any other character. In most of the dreams he is a bad guy, behaving in ways that bother and/or threaten Nan. The frequency of his appearance was surprising to Nan, who said she could not think of anything in her current relations with Phil that might cause such dreams. She and Phil had divorced thirteen years earlier, after their last child had reached college age. Since then they had maintained a friendly enough relationship to be able to attend family gatherings together. When Nan had her accident he made no special effort to contact or visit her, though he did come to California a few months later on business, and they had a pleasant lunch together.

I asked Nan to describe Phil, and she said he was a very outgoing man with a dynamic personality, successful in business and a stern disciplinarian at home. Nan paused, then said something very interesting: "I always felt I was in his shadow." Nan had always been a more introverted person than Phil, inclined toward art and spirituality rather than the competitive world of business. She worked part-time as an art teacher at a local grammar school, and she was quite a good artist herself, but none of this was taken very seriously by Phil. In their marriage his qualities were the ones that received all the attention, while hers were effectively ignored. In her own words, she stood in the shadows of the marriage while he basked in the spotlight.

After their divorce Nan developed a new career that drew strength from the very abilities Phil had refused to acknowledge in her, and for thirteen years she had been on her own, free from his domineering influence. This is what made Nan's recent dreams so surprising to her—they made her feel like she was back in the marriage. Her tenth dream is short and to the point:

10. I dreamed Phil was back in my life (not a good thing) and I can't see or didn't see.

The inability to see echoes her second dream (chapter 1), when she's trying to find her forgotten baby and can't see anything. "Seeing" is a common metaphor for knowing or understanding something—"I see your point"; "My view on this issue is clear"; "Let's take a look at his plan."[16] In Nan's dream the abrupt reentry of Phil into her life is accompanied by a loss of her ability to see, which metaphorically suggests a loss of understanding or knowledge, a failure of her vision, a helpless sense of confusion. Particularly for an artist, losing the visual sense is metaphorically equivalent to losing one's capacity for creative expression and experience.

Why is Nan dreaming that Phil is back in her life? Does it have something to do with her current waking-life relationship with Phil? The answer is almost certainly yes, at least at one level. Dreams are constantly working over our feelings about the people we love and used to love; you can hardly go wrong in dream interpretation by paying close attention to themes connected to personal relationships in waking life. In Nan's case, however, I suspect such an approach would be less fruitful than one focusing on Phil as a reflection of her inner world. If we look at his character as shadow figure—as a metaphorical embodiment of fears and concerns within Nan's unconscious—we can make better sense of the frequency of his appearance and the troubling emotional effects on Nan. Phil metaphorically represents Nan's experience of being helpless, dependent, and uncared for. That was how she felt in their marriage, and that is what she thought she had left behind her. But the car accident changed everything; suddenly she found herself physically damaged, totally vulnerable, dependent for her basic needs on the mercy of strangers, and bereft of supportive care and nurturance. In this context Nan's many dreams of Phil showed how the worst fears from her past had been reactivated by her present trauma. What had lain in the shadows of her psyche for thirteen years now burst forth with distressing urgency. Dreams with the "Phil Is Back" theme were (at one level) giving metaphorical expressions to Nan's long-standing fear of becoming helpless, a fear she did not want to admit consciously but now, after the accident, could no longer avoid.

We have discussed earlier the power of traumas to revive past experiences of loss or suffering. Nan's dreams of her ex-husband show how a new trauma can force a person to confront the lingering emotional remnants of those past experiences. The Jungian notion of the shadow archetype suggests that, as agonizingly painful as it may be to face the vivid reminders of past sufferings, the opportunity is there for tremendous healing to occur—if the shadow elements can be reintegrated into the broader personality. We will see in chapter 9 what Nan's dreaming imagination made of that opportunity.

I Am the Shadow

The most disturbing dream I had in the weeks immediately following the September 11 terrorist attack came on the night of October 28, a Sunday, at around three in the morning:

I have some anthrax….I ordered it in the mail from my friend K.?….At first I'm going to shoot it….Like a missile….It's in the shape of several long thin rectangles, made of tofu….But then I get scared, and I think to myself what am I doing?….I want to get rid of it….But how, with-

*out getting caught?....I feel very anxious and guilty....How can I get rid
of the anthrax without it being traced to me?....I walk through a
strange city, past a canal or river, looking for places to leave it....But
anywhere I think to put it, I immediately think of how I'll get
caught....I'm aware of other anthrax scares, the police shutting down
whole streets, and it feels like they're closing in on me....*

Over the years I have come to recognize two distinct patterns in my shadow dreams. The first, more frequent pattern
involves my being chased by some sort of evil, malevolent being—
a monster, vampire, alien, murderer, or such—and being unable
to escape no matter how fast I run, how cleverly I hide, how violently I fight, how urgently I try to persuade my antagonist to let
me go. I had a lot of nightmares like this in high school and college, and it was only after reading some of Jung's works that I
began to make some sense of them. Since that time, whenever I
have this kind of nightmare I look carefully at who or what is
chasing me to see if I can find any insights into possible conflicts
or tensions between conscious and unconscious forces within me.

The second type of shadow dream occurs less frequently, but
when it does come it can be even more disturbing than a full-
blown chasing nightmare. In these dreams *I'm* the bad guy—
rather than being a helpless victim of attack, I am actively doing
things that are destructive, cruel, and immoral. The dream just
described, which I titled "How Can I Get Rid of the Anthrax?",
illustrates this second type of shadow dream. In this dream *I am a
terrorist*—I have procured some of the deadly biological weapon
anthrax, and I am making plans to shoot it in missile form.
Considering the emotional tenor of the time I had the dream,
when the country was in full panic over anthrax and terrorism, my
dream portrayed me as doing the worst possible thing an
American could be doing right then. In the dream I suddenly realize this, and I feel an upsurge of fear and guilt at the abrupt recognition of my own badness. How could I even have thought of such

a thing? How could I be so terrible and thoughtless? I frantically try to get rid of the anthrax, but I cannot. There is no way to rid myself of the taint of my evil intentions. As the dream ends I feel a sense of constriction and pressure, as the authorities are closing in on me, and I am running out of ideas.

When I experience one of these "I'm a bad guy" dreams, which happens maybe two or three times a year, the first thing I do is focus on the acute emotional reaction I have at the shocking discovery of my evil intentions and behavior. I ask myself, What exactly am I afraid of? Where is the guilt coming from? In this dream, it is pretty clear: I am afraid of being caught by the police, and having the rest of society know what I tried to do; I am afraid of the shame of being revealed as a "terrorist." My concern is exclusively for myself (I give no thought to the likelihood that if I secretly dumped the anthrax it would probably harm other people), and I am consumed with self-reproach for going so far with such a hateful plan.

These intense feelings of fear and guilt pervade the second part of the dream, overwhelming all other concerns. But what is happening in the first part, before the startling self-discovery? What precisely am I planning to do? Two things jump out at me. One is that I receive the anthrax in the mail from my friend K. He is one of my closest long-time friends, and throughout my life he has been an amazing source of new ideas and unusual perspectives; he also has a history of getting in trouble and being involved in secretive countercultural groups. If I receive something in a dream from K., it automatically has a dangerous feel to it, a sense of hidden hostility toward mainstream society. But, it also has associations of potentially opening up new ideas and new ways of looking at the world. K.'s presence in the dream is simultaneously reassuring and disturbing.

The other element that stands out is the tofu. What a strange, absurd little detail! My first thought was to the previous evening, when I had grilled tofu and sliced vegetables for my family for Sunday dinner. Everyone loved it, and I was especially pleased at how much the kids enjoyed such a healthy meal. I also thought of the jokes people make about tofu, as an emblem of California vegetarian-style culture—a culture that stands in rather defiant opposition to the meat-eating majority of mainstream American society. This idea about tofu as a countercultural food echoed the association of K. with countercultural ideas, and it led me to wonder if the dream was expressing something about socially deviant desires within me. True, at that time I felt somewhat out of step with the rest of the country; I was not as gung-ho about the war on terrorism as were the vast majority of Americans, and I had serious doubts about the wisdom of responding to September 11 with nothing more than a military counterattack. But the dream seemed to be pointing at something more personally urgent than political disagreements. In the dream I am planning to attack people with *anthrax*—could that choice of weapons be a metaphorical expression for something else going on in my life, something involving the "dangerous disease" of shadow energies and desires? Have I been doing anything since September 11 that has "terrorist" qualities?

Reflection on that question led to an unexpected realization. Most of my research and writing energy at that time was devoted to the study of September 11-related dreams, and I had been sharing my findings with people in a variety of settings—classes, writings, media interviews, conversations with friends, and so on. I believed (at the level of ego consciousness) that my efforts were a positive contribution to the community at a time of great crisis— but now I asked myself, What if they were not? What if I am wrong in thinking a greater awareness of dreams is such a valuable thing? What if paying closer attention to dreams is actually *damaging* to society, like a dangerous disease, like a terrorist weapon, like anthrax? My own words came rushing back to me, things I said in classes and articles and interviews about dreams having the power to challenge waking-world authority structures, dreams transforming people's worldviews, dreams looking past the status quo to envision new and better futures....My conscious intention in saying these things was always to help people, but now I could not deny that my intentions were also influenced by darker, more aggressive energies with a strongly anti-authority, countercultural, revolutionary bent. If I were really, really honest with myself, I would have to admit it: *What I am trying to do is destroy society as it now is.* That was my deepest fear, and also my greatest desire. That was my shadow.

Hmm, I said to myself at this point, big thoughts....Big, heavy thoughts, full of gravity and truth. Too heavy, I realized, for a dream of tofu. At the end of my reflections I came back to that funny little image, attracted by its lightness, its self-mocking silliness. Here I found some degree of comic relief from the dark revelations of my shadow. How dangerous can I be if I'm a tofu terrorist? Are bean curd missiles really a mortal threat to the American way of life? I smiled. The spell of gravity was broken, the tension released, the burden of exaggerated fear and guilt lightened. I knew the shadow was still there in all its rageful, aggressive, destructive potency, but now I understood it a little more clearly, with a little more sense of proportion. I even got a new sense of its power to stimulate healthy growth, in its connection to the pleasing image from the previous evening of my three children heartily chowing down on long, thin rectangles of grilled tofu. Perhaps I should give my shadow some credit for being a good cook!

As anyone who has followed their dreams over a long period of time knows, dealing with the shadow is a lifelong task. I am sure I will have more shadow dreams in the future, dreams of being chased, being a bad guy, and getting caught up in a variety of disturbing, distressing, consciousness-threatening experiences. But at least for now, after some reflection on this particular dream, I could enjoy a sense of the good creative energy that comes from realigning the dynamic relationship of conscious ideals and unconscious desires.

I want to close this chapter on "bad-guy dreams" with a voice of respectful dissent. The Jungian approach to dreams, with its emphasis on archetypal symbols and personal individuation, is widely used in contemporary caregiving practice, but it does have its critics. One of the critics who has been most helpful to my understanding of Jung is Johanna King, a psychotherapist who worked for many years at the campus student health clinic at the California State University at Chico. King used dream and nightmare material extensively in her clinical practice, so she knew from lengthy experience how valuable dreams could be in therapy and healing. However, she did not believe that all dreams were deep revelations of the inner self, nor did she think the primary function of dreaming was to raise repressed feelings from the unconscious into consciousness. King wanted to balance that inner-oriented view (most commonly associated with Jung, but also found in the thinking of many other dream researchers) with appreciation of the outer-oriented view that dreams can also be reflections of, in her words, the *"dreamer's waking-life experience, and the dreamer's relationship, psychological and physical, to that waking experience."*[17] If a person has a dream about being attacked by someone, maybe it's not just a symbolic expression of deep inner conflict—maybe it's about a real waking-world fear of being attacked by that person. King warns that applying the interpretive framework of Jungian archetypes without due attention to the waking-world circumstances of the dreamer is misguided and potentially damaging.[18] As evidence of this, she points to a variety of people—sexual abuse victims, soldiers in wartime, torture victims, Germans living in Nazi Germany in the 1930s, survivors of the Jonestown religious suicides in 1978—whose dreams give extremely vivid portrayals of their painful waking-world experiences:

> All of these dreams, and many other less dramatic ones, make *primary* reference to the waking life circumstances of the dreamers and illustrate, I hope, how unbalanced or premature focus on the intrapsychic can sadly miss the dream message. In striving to understand and work with these dreams, we must be willing to look at and engage the ugly, disturbing, dark parts of the *world*, without mislabeling them as projected shadow, repression, or any other intrapsychic construct. If we fail to do this, we lose the opportunity each dream provides to 1) see the waking experience more clearly, frequently from a new perspective, 2) better understand the complex network of connections between the dream and waking experience, and 3) enable the dreamer to envision being in the situation, and in the world, in a different, new, enhanced, or more constructive way. Only when we explore these opportunities can we begin to really access the remarkably perceptive and creative ability of the dream state to envision both problems and solutions in the world. These problems and solutions can never clearly be visualized from a purely intrapsychic perspective, which too often emphasizes *internal* changes and adjustments, not changes in the world. Insight, self-awareness, and positive affective states do not by themselves produce contextual change.[19]

For anyone using dreams in a caregiving context, King's comments are worth taking very seriously. King's extensive clinical experience has given her an appreciation of both the benefits and the limitations of a strictly intrapsychic, inner-directed approach to dreams. She recognizes the tremendous creative power of dreaming, but she argues that an exclusive focus on self-development will not be enough to solve the large-scale social problems facing the world. Indeed, she is concerned that too much indulgence in narcissistic contemplation can actually drain people of the energy that's needed to deal with bigger problems. She has heard claims that it is not a zero-sum game, that intrapsychic reflection does not automatically lessen people's social or political involvement. King says, "I would like to be convinced by these optimists, but I worry."[20]

I share King's worry—and I go on with the work. I remain acutely mindful of her cautions as I continue to explore the inner-oriented shadow dimensions of dreaming. I seek the deep archetypal roots of bad-guy dreams even as I try to identify their connections to waking world experiences, and I try to be alert to the emergence of new creative energies in both personal and collective manifestations. There are no certainties in working with dreams, no way to be absolutely sure you aren't off on a wild goose chase. That fact is the ultimate shadow of dream interpretation, the dark antagonist looming over all our efforts, forever haunting anyone who seeks to learn from the elusive wisdom of the dreaming imagination.

Essential Bibliography

Dower, John. 1986. *War Without Mercy: Race and Power in the Pacific War.* New York: Pantheon.

Ellenberger, Henri. 1970. *The Discovery of the Unconscious.* New York: Basic Books.

Jung, C. G. 1965. *Memories, Dreams, Reflections.* Trans. R. and. C. Winston. New York: Vintage Books.

———. 1968. *Man and His Symbols.* New York: Dell.

King, Johanna. Let's Stand Up, Regain Our Balance, and Look Around at the World. In *Among All These Dreamers: Essays on*

Dreaming and Modern Society, ed. K. Bulkeley. Albany: State University of New York Press.

Notes

1. Personal communication, 9/26/01.
2. Beth also mentioned the following:

   Other dreams have involved crashing planes and that sensation of falling that sometimes comes in dreams which wakes me up. Luckily, the dreams have faded lately and I am sleeping with less interruption. Or at least only the interruption from the kids [Beth was the primary caregiver for her two children, ages five and one]. I think one of the things that has been hardest about this tragedy is the contrast between my happiness, indeed joy, about my private little days with my children versus the dark events of September 11 and worries about the future. The dreams seem to express this contrast with the image of things suddenly going wrong. (Personal communication, 9/26/01)
3. Personal communication, 9/28/01.
4. Ellenberger 1970. Myself, I would add to Ellenberger's story the even earlier influences of Augustine, Luther, Shakespeare, Descartes, and Kierkegaard on current Western psychological thinking about consciousness and the unconscious.
5. For Jung's version of events, see Jung 1965, chap. 5.
6. Jung 1965, 87–88.
7. William Shakespeare, *The Tempest*, V.i.275.
8. Jung 1968, 73. Italics in original.
9. Dower 1986.
10. Dower 1986, 145–46.
11. Dower 1986, 116–17.
12. Dower 1986, 309.
13. One good way of achieving this caregiving goal is to enhance people's historical awareness. I do not, of course, recom-

mend giving history lectures to people suffering the acute symptoms of PTSD. But I do, following the broad definition of caregiving I have used in this book, suggest that drawing greater attention to relevant historical experiences can be an effective method of strengthening people's capacity for meaning-making in times of crisis and confusion. This is another reason I find the works of Jung and Dower so valuable, because they help identify a variety of important symbolic connections between the histories of particular individuals and the histories of whole communities.

14. Dower 1986, 294.

15. Robert F. Worth, in an article titled "A Nation Defines Itself by Its Evil Enemies" (*New York Times*, 2/24/02, WK 1, 7), quotes Dower as saying the following about President Bush's State of the Union Address, in which he referred to Iraq, Iran, and North Korea as an "Axis of Evil": "Why has that phrase, 'axis of evil,' crystallized so much anti-American sentiment around the world? Because the country sees itself as nothing but good and innocent, and that infuriates people." Worth also quotes Eric Foner, a historian at Columbia University, as saying, "It is an unfortunate recurring pattern in American history. We have a tendency in times of war to adopt a Manichaean vision of the world. It's a state of mind that makes us demonize the enemy and leads to a failure to see dissent as anything but treason." Worth concludes the article by saying, "Ultimately, of course, terrorism does present a real threat, just as cold-blooded killing presents a moral outrage. But the history of American crusading, even against unmistakable evil, suggests that it can be more effective to start from a position of humility. Righteousness easily becomes self-righteousness, and it can be hard for crusaders to distinguish between the two."

16. Thanks to Bill Domhoff for this point.

17. King 1996, 226. Italics in original.
18. King 1996, 229.
19. King 1996, 234–35.
20. King 1996, 228.

7. War and Protest

Crises of Conscience

The events of September 11 gave rise to many different emotions. Shock, horror, disbelief, fear, sadness—for many people it was not just the intensity of their feelings but the bewildering multiplicity of different emotions that made the terrorist attack such a devastating experience. The confusing turmoil of the outer world was more than matched by the confusing turmoil of the inner world. Perhaps the most troubling emotion of all was the extraordinary rage that many Americans felt toward the perpetrators of the attack. Ordinarily mild, peaceable people found themselves suddenly swept up by an urgent, angry desire to strike back at the terrorists, to do violence to them, to make them suffer like we have suffered. Three weeks after September 11, the U.S. military launched a massive counterattack, with nearly unanimous public support. The Taliban regime in Afghanistan was the first target of American wrath, and while the campaign was justified as necessary to future U.S. national security, there was among many Americans a palpable sense of vengeful satisfaction at the destructive success of our powerful, high-precision bomb and missile attacks on the Taliban.

In provoking this volatile mix of aggressive emotions, September 11 is similar to many other types of crisis and disaster. Indeed, any kind of human-caused trauma (a war, a criminal assault, an act of terrorism) can spark extremely angry feelings against the people who caused the trauma (the enemy, the criminal, the terrorist), leading to vengeful acts of violent retribution.[1] The psychological and spiritual challenge facing people who have suffered these kinds of trauma is to distinguish their legitimate need for safety and security from the purely revenge-oriented desires to make their antagonists suffer. This, I would suggest, is also the challenge for caregivers who are trying to help people put their lives back together after an unexpected disaster. How best can we deal with those feelings of extremely violent rage? Do these feelings have any place in the healthy functioning of the human psyche? Even if we are perfectly justified in feeling intensely angry, aren't we still in danger of being carried away by such powerful emotions? When anger leads us to commit murderous acts of retribution, then it is truly self-defeating, for it merely adds to a cycle of violence that will ultimately come back to destroy us as well as our enemies. But at the same time, if the raw passion of outrage is immediately repudiated as somehow "not civilized" or "inappropriate" or even "unreligious," then we lose the essential emotional fuel that helps drive our ongoing struggle for greater justice, civility, and tolerance in the world. Here again, I believe the art of caregiving involves the ability to honor people's deep feelings of anger at the same time as we try to channel those feelings in creative, life-affirming directions.

Looking at a set of dreams relating to these issues reveals new dimensions of emotional complexity in people's reactions to September 11. The dreams offer a kind of symbolic mirror of the turbulent wartime passions of the American public in the weeks following the terrorist attack. In this chapter I suggest that paying careful attention to dreams like these can be of great practical value for caregivers who are trying to help people reorient their moral and spiritual values in times of war, violence, and bloodshed. As historian John Dower pointed out in chapter 6, warfare has the terrible power to overwhelm conscious awareness with bloody-minded thoughts and hateful fantasies of causing pain to

our enemies. This was true for our country in past military conflicts, it is true in the aftermath of September 11, and it will likely
be true in future wars as well. The angry, vengeful passions that
erupt during wartime can never be eliminated completely (nor
should they be), but they certainly can be understood more clearly
and honestly, and they can be more constructively integrated into
conscious awareness. Dreaming is a valuable ally in this process,
and almost any form of caregiving practice can be enriched by
exploring dreams as a means of insight into people's emotional
experiences during times of violent conflict.

An unusually public expression of war-related dreaming
appeared in an op-ed newspaper column written by Ruth Rosen,
an editorial writer for the *San Francisco Chronicle*. On October 22
Rosen wrote a column titled "Dreams of War and Peace," and she
opened with a frank confession of how disturbing her dreams
were in the weeks following September 11:

My dreams reveal the emotional and intellectual turbulence I try to con-
tain during the day. In one dream, I find myself in Afghanistan—
watching the bombing, praying civilians won't be killed. My editor calls
on a cell phone (which I don't have) and asks, "What are you doing
there?" I have no idea, I tell him. In another dream, I am on the West
Bank, just as Israeli soldiers shell a Palestinian neighborhood. Suddenly,
I see a group of teenagers strap bombs around the waist of a young man.
I scream at everyone to stop the killing.[2]

Rosen's dreams place her in two places of extremely violent
conflict, Afghanistan and Israel, where she is directly confronted
by the deadly, destructive realities of the current moment. I heard
many similar dreams following September 11, and the individuals
were often emotionally shaken for days after experiencing the vivid
dream feeling of *really being in a war*. We may read about war in
newspapers or see images of it on television, but certain dreams
have the power of creating an intensely realistic experience of what

it *feels* like to be caught in a war. Rosen prays for no more killing in her first dream, and screams out the same desire in the second, but in neither case is there any sense that her cries have any effect. In her column Rosen wrote that her dreams reflected her general feelings of moral confusion about the best way for America to respond to September 11—"Very little is clear, as my dreams keep reminding me."[3] As a politically liberal editorial writer she was accustomed to advocating positions on U.S. foreign policy that differed drastically from those of President Bush and his Republican supporters. But now, following the terrorist attack, she found herself haunted by her dreams and wondering how to relate her past ideals to the shockingly uncertain conditions of the present:

> These are difficult days. For some of us, whose lives were seared by Vietnam, the task is to yank ourselves from the past and confront an unprecedented and disorienting conflict. One by one, old friends confide that they support a carefully targeted military action against terrorists and the Taliban. One woman, a devoted Buddhist, tells me she is shocked by her thoughts and feelings. "I don't even kill ants or spiders in my house. Yet, I find myself supporting some kind of limited military response to terrorism." Another friend, who has long supported Third World liberation movements, calls to tell me that she, too, supports a military campaign against terrorism.[4]

A similar kind of moral and political shifting occurred among numerous Americans following September 11. Millions of people who voted against President Bush in the 2000 election were enthusiastically supporting his decision to attack Afghanistan after September 11. Like Rosen and her friends, many of these people were puzzled by the unexpected turn in their feelings and the surprising strength of their agreement with

President Bush and the military campaign. A good example of this moral and political shift is reflected in the dream of "Karen," a thirty-six-year-old lawyer from New York:

In the dream, I'm married to George W. Bush. We're hosting a birthday party for one of our children. At breakfast the next morning he does something to mess up the timing of the party, and I'm angry at him. I say some nasty things to him about his incompetence, but so only he can hear; in front of the kids I put on a good face. Later after breakfast I feel guilty, and worry that he won't forgive me. I got to apologize to him, and he's nice and says it's fine. Later, I see Barbara Bush, in a private setting behind the house, and Barbara gives me a present, like a welcome to the family. After that, George Sr. gives me a gift, also in private. I think about how unusual this gift-giving practice is, doing it in private rather than in front of others.[5]

Karen is a lifetime Democrat who bitterly opposed the candidacy of George W. Bush in the 2000 presidential election. She delighted in reading Molly Ivins's searingly critical biography *Shrub: The Short But Happy Political Life of George W. Bush*, and she had little respect for the new president's leadership abilities. But after September 11, Karen's feelings changed dramatically. She was not in New York when the attack occurred, but she knew dozens of people who were involved, and as a frequent air traveler who spent lots of time in tall Manhattan office buildings she felt the attack was aimed specifically at people like her. That feeling was magnified by the fact that she is a woman, and Jewish. Although she still disagreed with many of Bush's policies (indicated by her critical comments in the dream), Karen found herself agreeing wholeheartedly with the forceful approach the President and his circle of advisors were taking in Afghanistan. Her "new relationship" with President Bush is reflected in the dream image of being married to him: she has moved past her anger at his incompetence, and she is now being welcomed into the "Bush family."

On the Side of the Enemy

Not everyone experienced this shift of political allegiance, however. Some people who were critical of President Bush and his conservative supporters before September 11 became even more worried after the terrorist attack. Not only did these people feel deep misgivings about the military counterattack against Afghanistan, they also watched with alarm as a variety of new "homeland security" measures were imposed in the United States, with little consideration of their impact on constitutional liberties. Worst of all, they felt scared of their own disagreement with the majority—anyone who questioned the president or his policies risked being condemned as a traitor by an American public more passionately aroused and intolerant of political dissent than at any time in recent memory. "Mena," a thirty-eight-year-old business consultant from Virginia, felt herself in such a bind: "One of my strongest fears after the attacks was that freedoms in the U.S., and especially the freedoms of folks in any way associated with 'the Left' would be curtailed. Would people with any known liberal tendencies be targeted? Silenced? Worse? Did I need to start worrying about what mailing lists I was on, where I shop, etc.?"[6]

On October 25, Mena had this dream:

We're in some kind of military area, or maybe the military has taken over the area, the town, and they are rounding up citizens and taking them to be killed. It doesn't seem that there's any way to escape, they're just rounding up everyone. (Can't explain why the head of the military is from "our" country, not another; I think somehow they've decided it's necessary due to whatever is going on in the war we're in with our enemy.) I am filled with anxiety at knowing I'm going to be captured and killed, and that there is really no escape. I go into the adjoining room, and decide to hide in the closet hoping against hope that when they come into the house somehow they won't look there—the house will seem

*empty, and they won't realize I'm missing. A bit of a vain hope I think,
but the only one!*[7]

Mena saw the dream as a natural, dramatic extension of her fears of the political fallout from September 11. The image of her hiding in a closet hoping she won't be found is a perfect metaphorical expression of her concerns in waking life about losing basic American freedoms. Mena noted with some relief that in a dream a couple weeks later she is also being chased by someone, but this time she finds a place to hide that's much bigger and safer, and she's not nearly as scared of being found. Thinking about this shift from one dream to the next, Mena (who had some previous experience with dreamwork) said, "This actually seems to me to follow the notion that post-traumatic dreams attempt to integrate the trauma-related fear within a larger context of one's life and to get perspective on it."[8]

Other people who felt strong disagreement with the country's rightward political turn and who did not share the majority's enthusiasm for the bombing of Afghanistan had dreams that placed them among the enemy, that is, those people who were on the receiving end of U.S. military aggression. Here is a dream from Gerhard, a thirty-six-year-old teacher in Arizona:

*Last night I dreamt of being in an overrun country and being forced
with a large group of my people to stand on stage and sing an anthem
(perhaps "God Bless America"). It was like an Auschwitz "selection,"
those failing to measure up were condemned to death in some kind of
bombing. Later somehow I was on the ground, watching the huge, ray-
like jets swoop and soar and drop their bombs. We all stood, dumbly, as
these incomprehensibly advanced machines rained death upon us. Death
came in the form of small, clear disks, falling like party favors. They did
not explode at first and I picked one up, throwing it away from me,
knowing it would soon make a crater of my entire town, but powerless to
stop the impulse.*[9]

When Gerhard first told me this dream he commented that it struck him as surprisingly consistent with his waking views about the war in Afghanistan. I asked him if he could say more about that, and here is how he replied:

> I was pleased to see that my dream, an expression of my unconscious, was in harmony with my espoused views, expressions of my conscious, on the current war in Afghanistan. I am consciously, as you know, extremely wary of using violence to further political aims, even humanitarian ones. And I'm particularly averse to it in the Middle East. So my emotional sympathies lie with the hugely unfortunate, even pitiful people of Afghanistan. They are the ones having death rained down on them from nearly magical, fearful, ray-like stealth bombers and suchlike. And they—and to a certain extent we, too—are being judged on how well we snap to attention and show and sing how much we want God to bless America….It was a relief to me, in a sense, to have this dream. To see that perhaps I *don't* protest too much. To see that, at least that night, my unconscious experience remained sympathetic (literally) with, allied with, the bombed people, not with the bombers. In other words, I was happy that if dreams are wish fulfillments, this one was not a wish for revenge or power (in that case I would have been *dropping* the bombs), it was a wish to stand with the suffering of humanity and have the bombs dropped on me. Not only that, I was happy to see it express unconsciously my already consciously expressed feeling that we in America are being manipulated into a narrow, dangerous, my country right or wrong jingoism that is a mild form of colonization and oppression. In fact, it's

my suspicion that *this* is where the dream's power comes from. It comes from my own experience of being unheard and unvalued, of being forced to sing bilious pseudo-sacred hymns designed to turn my diverse nation and diverse self into an unquestioning war machine ready and willing to accept without question the decisions of the military running the show. So the manifest dream content concerns the experience of the Afghans and reflects my conscious views, but really is just symbolic of my *personal* experience, which is like theirs. I've thus chosen the dream because it is such a perfect screen on which to project my own inner war.[10]

Whether or not you agree with his political views, Gerhard's eloquent comments illustrate another important function that dreams can serve in times of crisis and conflict. When people have been struck by a terrible disaster and are trying desperately to rally their energies so they can face the challenges ahead, dreams often come that have the effect of reaffirming the deep integrity and worthiness of the people's efforts. These "reassurance dreams" can be thought of as the psychological opposite of shadow nightmares: while shadow nightmares bring rejected energies of the unconscious into conscious awareness, reassurance dreams confirm the deep authenticity of the individual's conscious ideals. It's as if the dream were saying, "Yes, that's right, you really *do* feel that way, and your feelings are *good* and *right*, even though the rest of the world disagrees with you." For Gerhard, this reassuring image of harmony between his conscious ideals and unconscious sympathies became an opportunity for him to reflect on what he was doing (and not doing) in waking life to act on those ideals. He said the dream "makes me more conscious of being so deeply disaffected with my own country…and it makes me feel more weak and lazy for not being out on the barricades in protest."[11]

Family Battles

One more example of a "war and protest" dream highlights a theme that is woven into many different types of dream experience: the dreamer's relationship with his or her parents. This is one of the places where Freud's ideas, for all their failings, are actually quite helpful. Although Freud's dream theory is often thought to revolve exclusively around a hunt for symbols of repressed sexuality, I think a better way to understand his psychoanalytic approach is to see it as a means of understanding and exploring the tangled emotional relations each of us has with our parents, the people who are the original sources of care, conflict, authority, and guidance in our lives. Many of Freud's patients were struggling to escape the oppressive influence of their parents and develop a stronger, more autonomous sense of personal identity. Freud's approach to treating these people drew heavily on dream interpretation as a means of identifying the unconscious conflicts generated in the natural course of all child-parent relationships.[12] In Freud's later cultural writings *(The Future of an Illusion, Civilization and Its Discontents)*, he expanded on those clinical insights to argue that people's early relations with their parents can have a profound impact on their feelings later in life about art, religion, politics, and morality. For example, people who worship "God the Father," who support father-figure political authorities, and/or who advocate the moral virtues of female chastity are all, in Freud's view, symbolically playing out their personal conflicts with their parents in a broader cultural arena.

I don't think Freud is completely right about this—not *every-thing* about our religious, political, and moral beliefs can be analytically reduced to symbolic expressions of child-parent dynamics—but he is right enough to be helpful in reflecting on a dream like this one, from "Michelle," a twenty-seven-year-old student in a health care graduate program:

I was at my grandparent's house in Nebraska—a bald headed eagle flew over and landed on the window right in front of me—BEAUTIFUL—Big bold—very powerful—I wanted to get closer to it, but as I studied it further, it formed a red aura around it. The aura became brighter and brighter until it started glowing. The eagle snarled at me and flew away—but an apparition of a joker like face was left behind—mime white—red everywhere—red eyeliner—bright red lipstick—red out-line—the eyes glowed red—VERY EVIL—laughing hysterically—then the eagle flew back and the face alternated between eagle and evil until it was pure evil—I couldn't have been more scared at that moment! The face's apparition became a solid figure and beamed glowing YELLOW light at me—I was surrounded by the yellow light. After that, every-thing I touched, even looked at was destroyed—I broke chairs—win-dows—bookcases—tornado valley to a tee, and I couldn't rid myself of the surrounding yellow light—the apparition laughed harder and harder as I destroyed more and more objects—My mom came into the room—I was afraid she'd drop to her knees at the chaos in the room...I tried franti-cally to explain what was happening—it's evil—evil—I can't stop it—I don't know what to do! She started crying and said the SAME thing happened to her—knowing that we were in this together—I told her not to be afraid—we've got to be strong and we'll be able to destroy it—the moment I said that—I had a VERY quick glimpse of Jesus—a flash—I'm not sure if it was his face—voice—presence—don't know what it was—but I remember the feeling—and with that the yellow light disap-peared—the chaos ended—and I woke up....[13]

Several things are going on in Michelle's dream. A few months before September 11 she read a report about U.S. mili-tary policy called "Future Warfare: America's Military Preparing for Tomorrow,"[14] and it deeply disturbed her. She was shocked to discover that elaborate plans were being made by the U.S. military to ensure the safety of America's global interests without any open discussion about what exactly those interests were. "Since the time I was first exposed to this article, I've really been questioning our and our government's values—and questioning 'what IS freedom?' and 'how DO we protect that freedom.'"[15] Michelle's skepticism toward the patriotic righteousness she perceived in everyone around her after September 11 is vividly reflected in the image of the evil bald eagle, a terrifying dream inversion of the U.S. national symbol: "Although I feel that the most beautiful aspects of the Eagle are its power, strength, pride…I also feel as though they're the most malevolent ones, especially when superiority and dominance come into play."[16] Thinking of this in terms of Jung's notion of the shadow, the menacing image of the evil bald eagle can perhaps be seen as a national symbol—a symbol of the dark, violent impulses seething and swirling in the unconscious of the nation.

After Michelle makes the terrifying discovery of the eagle's evil nature, she suddenly starts acting destructively herself—smashing chairs and windows, breaking everything in sight, while the "apparition" of the evil eagle laughs hysterically. When Michelle reflected on this strange shift in the dream, she came to a humbling realization. In the days immediately following September 11 Michelle, like many of us, received dozens of e-mail messages in which people voiced their feelings of raw anger at the terrorists, at Arabs, and at Muslims generally. Michelle vigorously opposed these people—she said, "I agree wholeheartedly with Barbara Lee,"[17] the California congresswoman who was the lone dissenter when the U.S. House of Representatives voted to support President Bush in a military response to September 11—and she could not help e-mailing back with equally vehement arguments about the dangers of self-righteous, out-of-control American militarism. Michelle had her dream on September 20, and the more she thought about the image of her smashing everything in sight, the more she realized how "militantly" she had herself been acting: "Instead of thinking rationally I've been bombing off e-mails regarding my views, not only to the people who send me those e-mails, but to the people on their mailing lists as well—so much for the humility and patience I'm trying to preach. I'm so focused on getting my own views out—thus 'wiping out' any other views—that I'm losing sight of myself. I'm preaching how we ought not focus on blaming—all the meanwhile pointing my fingers at our government."[18]

In this way her dream not only points to shadow issues in her community, but also to conflicts with her own personal shadow. It reminds me of my dream of being an anthrax terrorist (chapter 6) in having an "*I'm* the bad guy" narrative structure, and in forcing the humbling realization that what I most dislike in others is actually a part of me, too.

This is the moment in Michelle's dream when her mother enters the scene. She and her mother were, in waking life, in strong disagreement about the U.S. military response to September 11. Michelle's mom was "extraordinarily patriotic at this point—her views are far different than mine."[19] A year earlier Michelle had moved away from her family's home in Nebraska to go to school in California, and this made her historically troubled relationship with her mother even more difficult to maintain. In the dream, though, Michelle and her mother find something in common, something that opens up a new dimension to their relationship. Despite their waking-world political disagreements, Michelle's dreaming imagination reminds her of the potential for a deeper emotional connection between them. In the dream they share experiences of *suffering*, of being weak, vulnerable, and despairing, and somehow this realization enables Michelle and her mother to join together in common cause against the malevolent forces attacking them.

The emotional impact of this experience of reconnection with her mother is further intensified by the sudden glimpse of Jesus, which is immediately followed by an easing of the chaos, and then the end of the dream. Whenever an explicitly religious figure like Jesus appears in a dream, it is definitely worth the effort to ask the dreamer to say something about his or her religious upbringing and current religious beliefs. I asked these questions of Michelle, and she replied that was raised as a United Methodist, the denomination of her family, but rejected it and became an atheist as a teenager (this was a major source of her tensions with her mother). Then in college a friend introduced Michelle to a United Church of Christ congregation, and she "fell in love"[20] with it. Ever since that time she has been devoting much thought and prayer to the teachings of Jesus, trying to learn how to apply his ideals to her life. In her dream the flashing presence of Jesus stands in opposition to the evil bald eagle, reaffirming for Michelle the enduring vitality of her spiritual beliefs in the face of terrible challenges. The glimpse of Jesus also confirms the goodness of Michelle's emotional reconnection with her mother, and it brings a welcome sense of relief and peaceful closure after the frenzied, horribly frightening experiences of the first part of the dream.

Family relations, political protest, religious yearnings, revelations of the personal unconscious—Michelle's dream is as good an example as any of the intricate symbolic tapestries that are woven each night by the dreaming imagination.

Essential Bibliography

Rosen, Ruth. 2001. Dreams of War and Peace. *San Francisco Chronicle*, 10/22.

Notes

1. Rageful feelings are also likely to be stirred up by other kinds of trauma, such as "natural" disasters (floods, earthquakes)

and accidents (car and plane crashes, house fires). In such cases the angry vengefulness may be directed at scapegoats, that is, people who had nothing to do with the trauma but get blamed anyway, and/or at God, the ancestral spirits, or other religious figures.

2. Rosen 2001, A13.
3. Rosen 2001.
4. Rosen 2001.
5. Personal communication, 9/27/01.
6. Personal communication, 1/22/02.
7. Personal communication, 1/22/02.
8. Personal communication, 1/22/02.
9. Personal communication, 10/16/01.
10. Personal communication, 10/19/01.
11. Personal communication, 10/19/01.
12. An implication here (which Freud never pursued) is that the dreams of parents often revolve around emotional issues in their relationships with their children.
13. Personal communication, 10/23/01.
14. See www.dtic.mil/jv2020/index.html.
15. Personal communication, 10/25/01.
16. Personal communication, 10/25/01.
17. Personal communication, 10/23/01.
18. Personal communication, 10/25/01.
19. Personal communication, 10/25/01.
20. Personal communication, 10/25/01.

8. Anticipations

Did They See It Coming?

In addition to dreams that came after September 11, numerous people experienced dreams occurring *before* that day, dreams that in some strange way seem to have anticipated what happened. Many people (children as well as adults) had dreams before September 11 that contained scenes and images eerily similar to what happened in the terrorist attack on the World Trade Center towers. A few people had strikingly prophetic dreams the very morning of September 11, almost simultaneous with the actual event.

The question I address in this chapter is, What do we make of these accounts? Do dreams really have the power to foresee the future?

Before saying anything else about the subject, I want to start with the simple fact that a significant number of people have reported dreams that accurately anticipated key elements of what happened on September 11. This phenomenon is worth taking seriously, whatever ultimate explanation we may give for it, and caregivers who work with people affected by collective disasters like September 11 are likely to hear similar reports of dreams anticipating whatever terrible thing happened to the people involved. In this chapter I offer some ideas about how to respond to those reports, and I lay out the pros and cons of various explanations for them.

In most of my career as a dream researcher I have been skeptical toward claims of precognition in dreaming. Although I have had a couple of dreams that felt like anticipations of waking-life events (once a car accident, another time a child's illness), I have never been fully persuaded by the evidence used to support specific claims to precognitive dreaming. It is true that good, carefully controlled studies on paranormal dreams have been performed, and the results are intriguing.[1] But no matter how methodologically solid the studies are, conclusive proof of dream precognition remains elusive. The biggest problem is this: There is no way to rule out the possibility that a supposedly prophetic dream was just a coincidence. This is particularly true when the connection is made *after* the predicted event occurred. If a person has a strange dream, and then a strange waking-world event occurs, it is a natural (but logically fallacious) move to think there is a connection between the two, and to assume the dream *foresaw* the event. Even if a dream has imagery that relates very specifically to a subsequent event—for example, a dream of a plane crash followed by an actual plane crash—that still does not count as definitive proof of precognition. Every night countless people are dreaming of airplanes, and many of those dreams include images of planes falling and crashing. Knowing that fact, we can confidently predict that whenever a plane does crash, many people will indeed have dreamed it before it happened—not because of some mysterious power of precognition, but simply because of the law of averages.[2]

This is only one of the causes for skepticism. Another is the fact that people who publicly describe experiences of precognitive dreaming often receive valuable social attention in the process, producing a strong motivation to embellish or fabricate such reports.[3] More generally, a major obstacle to believing claims of precognitive dreaming comes from the recognition that all humans have a deep *wish* for the power of prophecy. The magical ability to predict the future is a prominent theme in countless myths, folk legends, fairy tales, and stories of all kinds, indicating how fervently people all over the world have desired such a power. The strength of this universal human wish is so great that even individuals of good credibility and character can be misled by their unconscious yearnings into believing in the reality of an ability that, in truth, is just a fantasy.

And even if claims of precognitive dreaming could somehow overcome these questions, the real problem comes in identifying the precise psychological means by which such an experience could occur. What part of the brain is responsible for seeing the future? Why do so few people possess this alleged ability for precognitive dreaming, while the vast majority of others don't? Why do prophetic dreams occur before some disasters but not others? Why are the dreams so rarely clear and direct in their predictions? Aren't they filled with as much wild symbolism and ambiguous meaning as any other kind of dream?

Perhaps the deepest problem with claims about dream precognition is philosophical: If people really can see the future in their dreams, does that mean we are all bound to a predetermined, unalterable fate? Does the power of precognitive dreaming ultimately deny the power of free will?

For anyone interested in pursuing the study of precognition in dreaming, these questions must be kept in mind. The bottom line is, there is at present no decisive evidence proving that dreams can foresee the future.

On the other hand, it should not be forgotten that there is no decisive evidence *disproving* the possibility of dream precognition either. The history of science is filled with the "discovery" of forces and phenomena that were not recognized by earlier generations of researchers and were dismissed as fantasies or random nonsense. This in itself suggests that along with our skepticism we maintain a sense of epistemological humility in our understanding of the world, never forgetting that what seems crazy and impossible to us today may be clearly understood and rationally explained by researchers some day in the future.

My own position at the moment is one of curious agnosticism. I do not yet see any convincing explanation of how dream precognition could work or how precisely it would fit into our current understanding of brain-mind functioning. However, the many reports we have of such dreams, from cultures all over the world and from all periods of history, remain deeply intriguing. Even if only a few of these reports are accurate descriptions of real phenomena, they would impel us to a dramatic revision of our view of the brain-mind system. With new discoveries being made every day about the astonishingly complex neuropsychological underpinnings of brain-mind functioning, right now is an especially poor time to set fixed boundaries to the full range and potential of the human psyche.

With all of that in mind, I would like to share the following brief reports of dreams that either came some time before the terrorist attack of September 11 or that came almost simultaneously with that day's events. After presenting the dreams I will return to the broader question of how reports of precognitive dreaming can best be understood in a caregiving context.

In the dream I am watching the Today Show on my TV and Katie Couric was talking. All of a sudden everything at the Today Show studio shakes and the TV signal from New York blacks out and immediately cuts back to local advertisements. I also feel my house shake a little bit in the dream because I live in Michigan and quakes in the Eastern U.S. travel for quite a ways. Then I see Katie talking about 10,000 people dying in a building. Either she is talking about the Empire State Building or the World Trade Center. In the dream the quake is very devastating because she can barely hold her emotions together on the air and in the background of the TV image I can see huge open spaces where tall skyscrapers once stood and one tall skyscraper billowing smoke from all of its broken windows.[4]

This dream came on July 29, 2001, and "Todd" (a forty-four-year-old man from Michigan) posted it on a Web site that afternoon, asking if anyone else had any similar premonitions. His initial thought was that it might portend a real earthquake in New York City, and he commented, "I usually don't write about dreams and I usually don't dream about far away places, but this dream stuck out because it scared the 'you know what' out of me."[5]

The following dream came to "Raphael," a forty-eight-year-old man from Pennsylvania on September 7.

I'm visiting a friend in the hospital. My friend is a young and healthy man completely unfamiliar in real life. The hospital is in a high-rise building in a big city. My friend's room is on a high floor, looking out over the city. Somehow I'm now a patient in the same place. I'm away from my bed when something strange happens. The whole building sort of shakes with a loud sound. The attendant says we all have to get out— evacuate the building. A day or so later, safely on the street outside, I'm reading a newspaper about a strange disaster. The article tells about a skyscraper building, part of which was a hospital, that gradually collapsed for no apparent reason, trapping and killing many people. At one point it identifies the building as "the tallest in Boston."[6]

The reference here is definitely more oblique, with several elements that differ from what happened on September 11 (for example, the setting of Boston rather than New York, the building being a hospital rather than business center, its collapsing for no reason rather than because of a hijacked airplane). But the dream did stand out in Raphael's mind when he woke up, and four days later when the terrorist attack actually occurred he couldn't help feeling he had somehow seen it coming in his dream.

On September 9, "Jean," a thirty-six-year-old woman from California had this dream:

I am in a high school auditorium. I am looking toward the stage, which has a movie screen. A burly-looking man in his forties wearing what looks like a ten-gallon hat walks across the screen. A person in the row ahead of me asks a woman walking up the aisle if there is going to be a memorial service. The serious-looking woman says that the family wants a private ceremony. I then find myself saying aloud, "Bye-bye, Daddy."[7]

Jean says that when she awoke she immediately felt it was not about her father, but about someone else's father. "I wrote it down, and I told many people the dream. I also hunted through newspapers to see if anyone resembling the man had died. I knew the man did not have an office job because of the way he was dressed."[8] Two days later, as Jean and the rest of the country watched the incredible TV images of the desperate rescue efforts at Ground Zero, Jean immediately associated the ten-gallon hat in the dream to the shape of the helmets of the New York firefighters.

A particularly striking report came to me from "David," a social worker in New York City, who had the following dream on Sunday, September 9, two days before the terrorist attack:

Several airplanes, one after the other, are taking off on a runway. I am the pilot who is next in line. I feel apprehension. I doubt my ability to steer the plane, because (even in the dream) I know that I am not really a pilot. I take off and my fear is confirmed. The plane rises, makes a curve and goes down crashing.[9]

David said the dream woke him up immediately, and he had a very unusual reaction to it:

> I remember "taking note," because this dream some-how seemed to stand out. I said to my wife, "I dreamt about a plane crash. Why did I dream about a plane crash?" Then I thought to myself, "Maybe there will be a plane crash." I put the thought aside and "forgot about it," until...two days later. The strongest image was the plane going down in a curve. The dream was kind of matter of fact, but I do remember feeling apprehension

as the pilot. I thought that it was unusual that the dream was so brief and circumscribed. I usually have longer, more convoluted dreams, especially when something terrible happens in them.

What is most intriguing about David's dream is its relation to an experience he had with his daughter a couple of days earlier:

> I think the dream about the planes may have been triggered by a visit to the World Trade Center on Labor Day, eight days before the disaster. I was with my four-year-old daughter and for the first time showed her the twin towers. I held her up with one arm and with the other I pointed at the towers. I felt a strange unease, almost anxiety, walking toward them. I clearly remember having had the thought: If these towers fell down, would they hit me and my daughter where we are standing now? The anxiety passed quickly though as we went shopping.[10]

In my conversation with David I was curious to hear how he would respond to the skeptical critique I have outlined, so I asked him what he would say about his experience to someone who didn't believe it possible for dreams to predict the future. He replied:

> I want to say that I am aware that nothing proves that the dream I had was precognitive. It may have been a pure coincidence. But I am glad you said that in such cases one also cannot disprove that it was precognitive either. If the dream was precognitive I think that the visit to the World Trade Center a week earlier with my four-year-old daughter may have played a role. This was my first visit with my daughter to this site. I think that the paternal instinct, the instinct to protect one's young

may have had something to do with it. We talk about "sensing that something is in the air." I do not have any explanation for feeling unease while walking with my daughter toward the towers. But I remember—without a doubt—at some point having the following thought: If these towers fell down, would they reach me and my daughter where we are standing now? In other words, are we far enough away from them if they fall or would they hit us? (Maybe it was because these towers really were kind of imposing and scary.)…I wonder if the key characteristic of people who dream about impending disasters is receptivity, more specifically, the capacity for empathy. Perhaps people like that, who can "tune in," are more likely to experience paranormal dreams.[11]

David's association between his dream and his waking experience with his daughter points to one possible answer to the question of what sets the precognitive dreaming process in motion. Before discussing that, however, let me briefly describe a handful of reports of dreams people experienced on the very morning of September 11. These reports cannot in a strict sense be regarded as precognitive. Rather, they are more precisely "synchrocognitive" (if I may coin such an inelegant term) in their near simultaneity with the terrorist attack.[12] The first is from "Bess," a thirty-one-year-old financial consultant who lives in rural Massachusetts:

At first I think I'm "watching" this, but then as the dream progresses, I'm in it. It's in some city, and there's a war going on. I see a lot of American soldiers (many young men), I think also civilians and soldiers of other countries running through the streets. People are very dense in the streets, and everyone's running, to get away from fire, presumably fire from bombs. Now I'm in the crowd, and as I'm running, I'm very aware of the presence of the fires behind me. I'm noticing different kinds of protective clothing the soldiers are wearing—some are wearing fire-retardant "boxes" which cover their torsos; some wearing other things. I think to myself that I've never been this close to war before. Then I'm in a building, several stories high up, still running down a hallway to an elevator, to get out. It's like an office building, the walls are white. It's just myself, and another woman also there running toward the elevator. We get onto the elevator, to go down, and just as the doors are closing I see a young girl with blond hair running, and I say this, and say we should hold the elevator for her. There's a young boy too. Maybe he is already on the elevator with us. I get the elevator door to open, the girl gets on, and the doors close. As we're waiting for the elevator to start going down, I go over to the girl and comfort her, put my hand on her head, and hug her. I realize as scary as this is for the adults, it must be much more terrifying for the children. Then the other woman does the same thing with the boy.[13]

Bess said the dream was "pretty unusual" for her, and when she woke up and saw on TV what was happening she felt her dreaming imagination had somehow "picked up on the collective unconscious knowing of what was about to happen."[14] She was particularly struck by the images of President Bush announcing the attacks from a grammar school in Florida, where he had been scheduled to visit that day. Bess said this magnified her "feeling that the very ending of the dream—with the emphasis on the importance of caring for the children—was both a collective as well as a somehow personal message to me."[15]

"Sue," a forty-three-year-old business consultant from Minnesota, described the following experience:

I am at some kind of air show, participating in a parade of planes on the ground. There are lots of onlookers, men, women and children running along the parade route. I am sitting in a convertible and look back at the plane behind my car. I notice two little boys running hand in hand and become alarmed that they are getting too close to the plane. As I watch, one of the boys trips and falls. His head is crushed beneath the wheel of the plane! I can distinctly see that his head is crushed on one side.[16]

Sue continued her account by describing what happened immediately after the dream:

I woke up from the shock, with the dreadful feeling that the events really happened. For some minutes I lay in bed wondering how I was capable of conjuring up such a terrible image. I noticed the time, 6:50 A.M. (MDT), about an hour later than I normally wake up. I decided to try to put the dream out of my mind as "just a nightmare" and got up. I went into my home office and turned on the radio and computer. As the computer was booting up I heard Bob Edwards on NPR say that one of the World Trade Center towers had been struck by a "commuter plane." I turned on CNN to see what was happening, saw the hole in the side of one of the towers and the smoke billowing up. Within minutes I saw the second tower being struck. At first I made no connection with the dream. Then it occurred to me: the two boys (twin towers), one boy's head struck by a plane (the top of a tower struck by the plane). But two towers had been struck. It was over an hour before I heard the report that the first tower had been hit at 8:45 EDT, that's 6:45 MDT. Allowing for a few minutes after I woke up, that's exactly when I dreamed about the boy's head being crushed.[17]

When Sue told a friend about her dream, he half-jokingly called it a "disturbance in the force" dream, referring to the scene in the original *Star Wars* movie when Obi Wan Kenobi (Alec Guinness) is physically stunned by the sudden destruction of a faraway planet, causing the death of all its inhabitants; Obi Wan says it's like he heard "a million souls crying out at once." Sue good-naturedly acknowledged the comparison; what she was describing certainly sounded like something out of a science fiction movie. But she had to admit that, as strange as it sounded, "my dream did feel that way except that the souls were condensed in the persons of the two little boys."[18] Indeed, even though she couldn't explain exactly how it had happened, Sue felt deep amazement and wonder at her dream: "It has been a life-transforming experience for me and is causing me to rethink all previous dream experiences and take them more seriously."[19]

I asked Sue the same question I asked David, namely how she would respond to a skeptic's disbelief in what she was describing. She answered that she was raised as a Christian Scientist, but rejected the religion in her twenties when her mother died of cancer despite the supposed powers of "spiritual healing"; and ever since then she had taken "a fairly skeptical attitude" toward life.[20] As a result, she could understand someone not believing her dream report:

> I can provide no evidence of my dream other than the telling of it. It did not happen enough in advance of the incident for me to report it to anyone. I was alone when I woke up. I can only say, why would I make up something that reflects so badly on the contents of my imagination? When I thought the dream was "just a dream" I was filled with disgust that I could imagine something so appalling. It has been rather difficult to talk about for that reason. I suppose skeptics would say I am torturing the symbolism of my dream to relieve myself of guilt for my terrible imagining and that the timing was mere coincidence. And I say, let them think what they want. I know what I dreamed and when I dreamed it and the

events that ensued. I know the effect the dream had on me; that's all that matters to me.[21]

In speculating about possible explanations for the phenomenon of precognitive dreaming, Sue was most interested in current research exploring the possible connections between quantum physics and human consciousness. If it is true, as investigators in quantum physics are suggesting, that ordinary physical matter is *not* the ultimate foundation of human existence, then it calls into question all models of psychological functioning that depend exclusively on the material operations of the brain. For Sue, this opens the door to new explanations of precognitive dreams and many other unusual states of awareness and experience.[22]

A final brief report comes from Gerhard, the Arizona teacher whose dream of being bombed with the people of Afghanistan was described in chapter 7. In addition to that dream, Gerhard said that in the weeks following September 11 he experienced several dreams in which he is a passenger in jets that smash into things and are likely to crash, and "the first of these dreams was early morning September 11, before being awakened to watch the reality on television."[23] However, Gerhard said that he and the others in his house were awakened that morning by a phone call, and while everyone else got up, turned on the television and watched the unfolding events, Gerhard remained in his bedroom and fell back asleep. Thus, he said it is certainly possible his plane crash dream could be explained as a subliminal perception while he slept of the television reports and his family's conversation, although he doesn't think this is what actually happened—"I truly do not believe this is the case, but hey, I was sleepy; I might be misremembering."[24]

Possible Explanations

The dreams reported by Gerhard and all the others in this chapter have no more or less credibility than any other kind of dream report. They are descriptions of subjective experiences that cannot be directly verified by an outside observer. Even if we trust the people's honesty and sincerity (that is, even if we believe they are not just making it up), there is always the possibility that unconscious influences have altered their conscious recollection of what happened. This means we are no closer than at the start of the chapter to having definitive evidence that precognitive dreaming is a real, scientifically verifiable phenomenon.

However, we have touched on several points that are worth further reflection. The first is that in each case the dream was experienced as unusually strong and memorable directly upon awakening, before any possible connection with a future event was considered. At a deep, visceral level of awareness the people felt something strange about these dreams, and many of the dreamers made a specific effort to talk about their experiences with friends and family members. This suggests the possibility that *if* any reports of dream precognition turn out to be legitimate, a distinguishing feature may be their unusual emotional intensity. Referring again to our airplane example, perhaps a truly prophetic plane crash dream would *feel* different, both in the dreaming experience and upon awakening, as compared to a normal, non-predictive plane crash dream.

A second potentially helpful point comes from David's speculation that perhaps forces of parental instinct and empathy are at work here. The primal desire to safeguard one's children from future danger is certainly a powerful motivator in human psychological functioning, and again it is reasonable to think that if precognitive dreaming does indeed occur, it might be "triggered" (as David says) by that parenting instinct. His mention of empathy also suggests that what might enable certain people to experience precognitive dreams is a heightened sensitivity to the psychological states of other people. The more open a person is to the subtleties and nuances of other people's inner lives, the greater is the possibility of perceiving information that can be processed by the dreaming mind into an accurate prediction of something about to happen. In this regard David compares the mind to a kind of radio that has certain powers of "receptivity" and an ability to "tune in" to invisible but meaningful signals.

Bess suggests a possible connection of precognitive dreaming to Jung's theory of the collective unconscious. Jung devoted great attention to synchronistic phenomena—events that are meaningfully connected in their deep symbolic meaning even if, in terms of contentional physical causality, they appear to be coincidental.[25] Perhaps precognitive dreaming occurs when an event of collective archetypal power is about to happen, and the potential danger of the impending event is so great that extraordinary psychological processes are activated in order to receive, process, and convey vital information. Sue's reference to quantum physics could be seen as complementary to Jung's in providing a new way of thinking about phenomena that seem to violate ordinary laws of time and space. Research in this area is still at a highly speculative stage of development, so I remain hesitant about accepting any quantum physics explanation as the final word on precognitive dreaming. Without a doubt, the discovery of subatomic dimensions of reality has revolutionary implications for our understanding of human consciousness. But my feeling is that right now, in the early years of the twenty-first century, we have only the tiniest glimmer of understanding of those implications, so the best thing to do is remain open-minded, apply the highest standards of skeptical analysis, and keep on with the research.

A Caregiving Response

What lessons should caregivers draw from this discussion? First and foremost, people who have suffered some kind of disaster periodically report dreams that seemed to predict the traumatizing event. Setting aside the different theoretical explanations for these dreams, the practical reality is that people are often puzzled and even troubled by such experiences. A strong sense of guilt, moral weakness, or failed responsibility can be generated ("If I really saw it coming in my dream, should I have somehow acted to prevent it?"), and this inevitably becomes part of the emotional dynamics of the caregiving situation. Indeed, the emotion of guilt is one of the most difficult to address in working with trauma survivors. On the one hand, the healing efforts must aim at diminishing an exaggerated sense of responsibility for the trauma, helping the people understand that what happened was *not* their fault. On the other hand, a full restoration of health cannot occur without honestly facing the sensitive question of how much partial responsibility the people *did* have for contributing to the circumstances that led to the disaster.

My approach to this caregiving challenge, and to reports of precognitive dreams generally, draws upon a deep appreciation of the power of human consciousness to anticipate future dangers. Even diehard skeptics will likely agree that mainstream cognitive science has convincingly demonstrated that a primary function of human consciousness is to generate imagined scenarios of the future in order to increase our chances for survival and reproductive success (this is the conceptual basis for Revonsuo's "threat simulation" theory of dreaming, discussed in chapter 3). The human mind is constantly pondering the future, imagining different possibilities for experience and action, and thinking through various strategies for achieving our goals. There is no magic or mystery to these cognitive processes—they are the stuff of our everyday mental experience. To realize this about the mind is to understand that we *do* see many things coming in the future, and thus we are always partly responsible for what happens to us. Humans have a tremendous ability to foresee the future, and over the course of our lives our brain-mind systems are continually working to improve the functional sophistication of our predictive powers.

But—we are not omniscient. Our perspectives are always limited, our understanding always finite. Here again, a degree of humility is required in honestly accepting the flaws and frailties in human life. We can see many things coming in the future, but we can't see everything. Although we fervently wish we could foretell the future, the fact is that we can't. Despite our many impressive cognitive abilities, sometimes things hit us that we just don't have the strength to stop. There is no moral breakdown in this, no failure of responsibility, just a humbling confrontation with our own limitations.

If a convincing explanation for precognitive dreaming is to emerge some day, I suspect it will build upon current cognitive psychological research in the areas of reasoning and imagination. Indeed, Revonsuo's work on threat simulation dreams shows how centrally dreaming is involved in the efforts of the mind-brain system to anticipate the future. And well before Revonsuo, Jung was speaking of the "prospective function" of dreaming, which draws its power from the associative processes of the unconscious: "The prospective function...is an anticipation in the unconscious of future conscious achievements, something like a preliminary exercise or sketch, or plan roughed out in advance....It would be wrong to call them prophetic, because at bottom they are no more prophetic than a medical diagnosis or a weather forecast. They are merely an anticipatory combination of probabilities which may coincide with the actual behavior of things but need not necessarily agree in every detail. Only in the latter case can we speak of 'prophecy.'"[26]

Thinking in terms of possible extensions of the anticipatory powers of the human psyche is, in my view, the best way to approach reports of precognitive dreams. All of the skeptical concerns remain—questions about coincidence, fabrication, wish fulfillment, self-deception, and so on—but ultimately each individual experience has to be evaluated and understood in its own unique context.

Perhaps in such a condition of uncertainty we should make a practical decision to dismiss all precognitive dream reports, because allowing people to believe even in the possibility of so fantastical a phenomenon does a disservice to their intellectual development. I appreciate the force of that argument, but my greater concern is that an all-encompassing skepticism will have the perversely self-fulfilling effect of actively suppressing the very phenomenon it claims does not exist. A great deal of research has shown that dream recall is sensitive to a variety of external influences, including personal attitudes. Here is sleep laboratory researcher John Antrobus's summary of the research:

> Dream recall is an implicit measure of one's memory of a dream. Recent memory research on brain-damaged patients, who have very poor recall of stimuli when awake, demonstrates that the more cues they are given, the more likely they will eventually recall the stimuli. Thus, one major reason for the failure to recall dreams appears to be the absence of cues in the waking environment that effectively help an individual recall the dreams of the previous night. Consequently, if relevant stimuli are encountered throughout the day, they will often cue the recall of a dream from the previous night.[27]

This is a pretty commonsensical finding. If people are encouraged through their waking day to pay attention to their dreams, they are likely to remember more of their dreams when they wake up each morning. This seems to be the case in many non-Western traditions around the world, where dreaming enjoys a much higher degree of cultural esteem and where people evidently have a higher degree of actual dream recall.[28] The flip side of this is that if people are encouraged *not* to pay attention to their dreams, and if they are told by authoritative figures that certain kinds of dreams *cannot* exist, their dream recall will almost surely be drastically diminished. I believe that kind of premature closure of human imaginative potential is the greatest danger of all, and so I always remain open to hearing people's stories of mysteriously accurate anticipatory dreams—even as I make sure to examine their reports with critical caution.[29]

I would like to end this chapter with a brief discussion of one of the most puzzling turns in the post–September 11 conflict, namely the homemade videotape released two months after the attack featuring Osama bin Laden, an unnamed sheik, and several other men discussing prophetic dreams and visions relating to September 11. When the videotape was released and played repeatedly on television, many commentators expressed condescending amazement at bin Laden's interest in such tribal superstitions—"The self-described holy warriors occupy a world in which dreams are omens."[30] But in fact the seemingly absurd conversation caught on the videotape is quite revealing of the deepest motivations guiding the behavior of bin Laden and his followers.

Dreams and visions have played an enormously important role in Islam from its very beginning.[31] The Prophet Muhammed is said to have received the first revelation of the Qur'an in a dream visitation from the angel Gabriel. Throughout his life Muhammed experienced dreams he believed were communications from Allah, and he encouraged his followers to tell him their dreams so he could interpret them. Many of these dreams included images of violence and warfare, and in each case the

169

dream was interpreted as a sign of God's support and guidance in the battle against the unbelievers.

Viewed in this light, the video portrayed a ritual reenactment of the dream interpretation practices of the Prophet Muhammed. Bin Laden, playing the role of the religious-military-political leader, was taking time out from the war against the infidels to speak with his followers about dreams, visions, and other reassuring signs that God was on their side and would guide them to ultimate victory. This is identical with what Muhammed practiced with his followers on a regular basis almost 1,400 years earlier, and the video is perhaps the clearest evidence yet found that bin Laden was patterning his life after the Prophet Muhammed and felt himself blessed with the same degree of divine approval for his violent struggle with the enemies of God. His perverse success in persuading thousands of young Muslim men to fight and die for him was very likely due to their perception of him as a Muhammed figure—an inspiring warrior-prophet who embodies the wrathful power of Allah.

Can anything be learned from the particular dreams discussed in the video? Bin Laden and his followers mention a total of seven dreams and dreamlike experiences. The first involves a strange soccer game between American airplane pilots and Muslim airplane pilots, which the Muslim team wins. Three other dreams portray airplanes crashing into tall buildings. A man is reported to have had a vision of carrying a huge plane on his back to the desert, while another man envisioned a group of Muslim faithful leaving for jihad in New York and Washington. Bin Laden says a soldier told him he'd dreamed of a tall building in America, and then of learning from a spiritual teacher how to "play karate."

Given the concerns I have expressed about the premature closure of human imaginative potential, I found it especially chilling to hear bin Laden himself describe a young man who dreamed, before September 11, of a tall building in America: "At that point," bin Laden tells his followers, "I was worried that maybe the secret would be revealed if everyone starts seeing it in their dreams. So I closed the subject."[32]

What is particularly striking about these dreams is how similar they are to the dreams reported by Americans in this chapter. Many of the American dream images are almost identical to the bin Laden dreams, but the emotions they evoke are radically different: the American dreams are suffused with fear, confusion, and a horrible sense of vulnerability, while the bin Laden dreams are welcomed as good omens. What terrifies the Americans brings joy to the Muslims. Nothing could make clearer the distressingly huge psychological gap separating the two warring sides.

Essential Bibliography

Antrobus, John. 1993. Recall of Dreams. In *Encyclopedia of Sleep and Dreams*, ed. M. A. Carskadon. New York: Macmillan.

Bulkeley, Kelly, ed. 2001a. *Dreams: A Reader on the Religious, Cultural, and Psychological Dimensions of Dreaming*. New York: Palgrave.

Hermansen, Marcia. 2001. Dreams and Dreaming in Islam. In *Dreams: A Reader on the Religious, Cultural, and Psychological Dimensions of Dreaming*, ed. K. Bulkeley. New York: Palgrave.

Irwin, Lee. 1994. *The Dream Seekers: Native American Visionary Traditions of the Great Plains*. Norman: University of Oklahoma Press.

Jedrej, M. C. & Rosalind Shaw, eds. 1992. *Dreaming, Religion, and Society in Africa*. Leiden: E. J. Brill.

Jung, C. G. 1968. *Man and His Symbols*. New York: Dell.

———. 1974. General Aspects of Dream Psychology. In *Dreams*. Princeton: Princeton University Press.

Krippner, Stanley, Fariba Bogzaran, & Andre Percia de Carvalho.

2002. *Extraordinary Dreams and How to Work with Them.* Albany: State University of New York Press.

Miller, Judith. 2001. A Glimpse, Guard Down. *New York Times,* 12/14.

Poe, Edgar Allan. 1981. *The Complete Tales of Mystery and Imagination.* New York: Octopus Books.

Scenes of Rejoicing and Words of Strategy for bin Laden and His Followers. 2001. *New York Times,* 12/14.

Stephen, Michelle. 1979. Dreams of Change: The Innovative Role of Altered States of Consciousness in Traditional Melanesian Religion. *Oceania* 50 (1):3–22.

Tedlock, Barbara, ed. 1987. *Dreaming: Anthropological and Psychological Interpretations.* New York: Cambridge University Press.

Van de Castle, Robert. 1994. *Our Dreaming Mind.* New York: Ballantine Books.

Notes

1. See Van de Castle 1994; Krippner, Bogzaran, & de Carvalho 2002.

2. I recently came across a passage in an Edgar Allan Poe story, "The Mystery of Marie Roget," that expresses this point about coincidence and chance with wonderfully gothic eloquence:

> There are few persons, even among the calmest thinkers, who have not occasionally been startled into a vague yet thrilling half-credence in the supernatural, by *coincidences* of so seemingly marvelous a character that, as *mere* coincidences, the intellect has been unable to receive them. Such sentiments—for the half-credences of which I speak have never the full force of *thought*—such sentiments are seldom thoroughly stifled unless by reference to the doctrine of chance, or, as it is technically termed, the Calculus of

Probabilities. Now this Calculus is, in its essence, purely mathematical; and thus we have the anomaly of the most rigidly exact in science applied to the shadow and spirituality of the most intangible in speculation. (Poe 1981, 382. Italics in original.)

The protagonist in Poe's story is the same one who solves the mystery of "The Murders in the Rue Morgue," a young man named the Chevalier C. Auguste Dupin, who periodically rouses himself from strange, unnamed nocturnal researches to apply the strict rules of logic to the explanation of especially horrifying acts of criminal violence.

3. Although, former Association for the Study of Dreams President and Executive Officer Rita Dwyer pointed out to me that the social attention can often have a negative tone. I sent Rita an early draft of the material in this book, and she replied as follows:

Since you asked, I'll make a few comments on the precog portion, since it intrigues me the most. I didn't realize you were such a skeptic toward precognitive dreaming, given all the reliable and credible accounts that can be found, but then I, too, am skeptical of some who make such claims. If it weren't for my own experiences, I'd probably be even more skeptical, though as you know I've become a believer, and am not an agnostic. When you write of the two factors that make it difficult for you to believe in certain accounts, I agree—there are certainly coincidences that are fairly amazing and there are those who would reap attention with their "powers" to see the future. However, there are also those who feel embarrassment, guilt, fear and anxiety about sharing these dreams, and the psi e-study group members often remark that they are happy to have a place where they can share these dreams without experiencing such negative emotions. Not everyone is looking for social attention, just some place to be heard and not scoffed or laughed at. I know how many years it took me to be able to speak of Ed's dreams that understandable given the hazardous research we did, and that is true at one level, the awesome sense of wonder and the need to understand such a mysterious and fateful occurrence which was generated in both Ed and me at a very deep soul level, is not so easily understandable nor even explainable. It's been luring me on for years now, but I am no closer to understanding nor explaining the brain-mind-soul connections that combine to bring us such dreams than when I started looking into them. I have heard enough valid accounts to know that such events do occur to very ordinary people who can't understand nor explain the theory or practice, either, yet believe they can and do happen, elicited or not. I, and these others, are quite content to use the dreams if they are truly precognitive, and to weed out those which are clearly our own psychological stuff, though both can be so entwined as to make that a difficult proposition. (Personal communication, 10/31/01.)

4. Personal communication, 10/1/01.

5. Personal communication, 10/1/01.

6. Personal communication, 9/24/01.

7. Personal communication, 10/8/01.

8. Personal communication, 10/8/01.

9. Personal communication, 12/23/01.

10. Personal communication, 12/23/01.

11. Personal communication, 1/2/02.

12. The terminology in this area of dream studies is still a work in progress. Other researchers might refer to the following dreams as "clairvoyant," but I do not think it is helpful to emphasize either the clarity of these experiences (because they usually are not terribly clear) or the visual sense (because dreams are always multisensory experi-

ences). The term "synchrocognitive" has the advantages of highlighting the temporal anomalies involved in these experiences and the role of cognitive, brain-based processes in their formation.

13. Personal communication, 9/11/01.
14. Personal communication, 10/2/01.
15. Personal communication, 10/2/01.
16. Personal communication, 9/28/01.
17. Personal communication, 9/28/01.
18. Personal communication, 9/28/01.
19. Personal communication, 9/29/01.
20. Personal communication, 9/29/01.
21. Personal communication, 9/29/01.
22. Here is another intriguing account, gathered by Anne Frey, a dream educator and workshop leader in Indiana, from a friend of hers who was living in Japan at the time of the attack:

> On another note Anne, you asked earlier for dreams related to Sept. 11. This maybe too late or not useful but I feel the need to share it (my husband would prefer I not!) My five-year-old daughter shared elements of a dream the morning after the attack (it occurred at 10:00 P.M. Japanese time). I often ask her to tell me what she was dreaming about but she doesn't usually remember anything. That morning of the 12th, I only mentioned very briefly that a sad thing had happened—that a plane has flown into a building and hurt some people. With no prompting whatsoever, she then proceeded to tell me about the planes (plural!) that she had dreamt about—that the people flying them were actually good people but some other people on the plane were bad and made them crash [I'm certain she hasn't learned consciously about the concept of hijacking]. With a storyteller's matter-of-fact

175

confidence, she tells me that those same buildings (I had only mentioned ONE building) "when they were younger had an earthquake in the basement" but that they "were OK" [she hears about earthquakes here—but wouldn't know about bombs!]. The next day, out of the blue, she volunteered to tell me more about her dreams. She said, with some confusion on her face (as though trying to describe something in her limited vocabulary that she could see in an image), that there were actually two levels of planes flying—the higher ones were good ones, the lower ones were bad.

Was she tapping into the subtle fields of morphogenic awareness—of heaven/hell archetype duality? I don't know but there were so many other things she was telling me that were "freaky" I wish I had written them all down—I can only remember the ones that stick in my memory as "truth" on some dimension—not just a child's creative fantasy. Luckily, my daughter is not at all disturbed by these dreams—even though psychologists say that children at her age shouldn't be exposed to news and discussion about traumatic events because they can't handle it! (Personal communication, 10-22-01.)

23. Personal communication, 10/16/01.
24. Personal communication, 10/19/01.
25. Jung 1968.
26. Jung 1974, 41.
27. Antrobus 1993, 492.
28. See Jedrej & Shaw 1992; Irwin 1994; Stephen 1979; Tedlock 1987; Bulkeley 2001a.
29. And I remain open to my own experiences. Here is the dream I had the night of Sunday, September 9:

I'm with two other guys, we're in an airplane, at an open door, looking down on an ocean and shoreline below.... We're being forced to play some weird game; jump off the plane, into the water, swim to shore, blend into a society that is all slaves, though the people don't know it....I look down, imagine the jump, and I'm scared....But somehow we get down there....Arnold Schwarzeneggar is part of the game, but I'm not sure if he's good or bad....We try to help the people get free....

30. Miller 2001, B4.
31. See Hermansen 2001.
32. Scenes of Rejoicing 2001, B4.

9. Visions of Hope

Life Beyond September 11

The dreams that follow an unexpected disaster are almost always filled with darkness, fear, and confusion. But in my experience even the worst nightmares have elements of *light*, too, elements of enduring strength, vitality, and creative energy. In the preceding chapters we have looked at numerous dreams combining dark, intensely nightmarish feelings with glimmers of real hope for the future. As I have suggested in discussing these dreams, caregivers should do what they can to help people acknowledge *both* dimensions of their emotional experience, because only in this way can they fully mourn their losses and move through their suffering into a new capacity for creative living. This is no easy task, to be sure. The two emotional dimensions can easily develop a mutual antagonism, like the opposite ends of a magnet—the feelings of terror and vulnerability can push away any sparks of renewed optimism, while the visions of hope may be so alluring they end up denying the harsh, painful realities of the present. But this caregiving challenge must be undertaken, because if either of these emotional dimensions is lost the healing process will ultimately fail. Of course, some people may forge hasty emotional compromises to regain at least a minimal degree of psychological functioning (for example, by totally defining one's identity as a "trauma victim," or alternatively, by pretending that the trauma never happened, the person is OK, everything is fine now, and so on). But these half-measures will never substitute for a full integration of both emotional dimensions, the horror *and* the hope, in the psyches of people who have been impacted by a sudden tragedy. As I have tried to show throughout this book, working with dreams is perhaps the simplest and most direct means of moving toward that healing synthesis.

One of the most common forms taken by dreams of hope and reassurance is the reappearance of a loved one who has recently died. A month after the terrorist attack a New York firefighter ("Dan") reported having a dream like this involving his firehouse roommate, one of nearly a dozen men from his company who died on September 11:

I was asleep in my dream, and my friend woke me up and told me that he was dead. He told me that I needed to go on.[1]

Dan found this dream strangely comforting, saying, "At least I knew what happened, even though I was still hoping."[2]

Some people might regard this dream as a Freudian wish fulfillment, in which Dan's mind has fabricated an image of his friend as still alive in order to assuage his sad feelings. It might *seem* like his friend came back, but really the dream was just a product of his own unconscious desires. Other people with a different theological or philosophical worldview might regard Dan's dream as a "visitation" in which the soul of the deceased friend actually returned to convey a valuable message, and then say a final farewell. As readers can probably guess by now, my view is that both explanations have an element of truth. However, I believe what is *most* important about such dreams is the emotional impact they have on the dreamer. Whatever the explanation of their ultimate cause, whether they come from deep inside the dreamer or from a spiritual realm external to the individual, the psychological effect of such dreams is almost always in the direction of new growth: replenishing the dreamer's emotional vitality, stimulating new energy for the future, and giving him or her the ability to get up in the morning, accept the losses of yesterday, and face the challenges of today. Dan's dream achieves this psychological effect with remarkably concise symbolic clarity. At the time he had the dream, Dan and most of the rescue workers at Ground Zero still nursed the hope that survivors—maybe even their friends and colleagues—might be found alive. Dan went to sleep one night during this time and had a dream in which his firehouse roommate wakes him up (in the dream) and reveals the painful but honest truth: Dan is not going to find his friend in the rubble of Ground Zero. In his waking life, Dan had been clinging to this desperate hope, but in his dream he is confronted with the stark, unavoidable reality of his friend's death. Given that Dan lived and worked in the same firefighter culture that Gloria Sturzenacker found was so disinterested in emotional self-reflection (chapter 2), my sense is that Dan's dreaming imagination made symbolic use of that waking-world disinterest for the specific purpose of making the dream's message more likely to catch his conscious attention. For someone who fundamentally believes that waking awareness is the only legitimate source of truth, what better way for a dream to express a vital *unconscious* truth than by imaginatively creating a scene in which the person "wakes up" to hear it? The deeper symbolic paradox in Dan's dream is that it both dashes his hope for the physical survival of his friend and yet stimulates new energy toward the future—*"He told me that I needed to go on."* The dream is both a sobering confrontation with the concrete facts of the present and an inspiring encouragement to continue working, striving, and reaching forward.

In this way the dream relates to many others, experienced by people all over the world, that feature the striking appearance of recently deceased friends and family members. In my studies of historical and cross-cultural dream patterns I have found this to be one of the most frequently reported types of "big dream," that is, those dreams that people experience with an extraordinary emotional power and imagistic intensity.[3] I have also found that in speaking to people in contemporary society, dreams of the dead are experienced with remarkable frequency. When talking about these dreams people almost always emphasize the intense *realism* of the dream, the way it really felt like the deceased loved one was right there with them. I remember a couple of years ago a woman asking me about the incredibly vivid sensations she experienced in a dream of her husband (who had died five years previously): They were dancing together, and she could *feel* the brush of his beard against her cheek, the smell of his cologne, the texture of his jacket under her fingers. Why, the woman asked me, would she have such an incredibly realistic dream like that? What was her mind trying to tell her? My reply was that, if it were my dream, the sheer *intensity* of the dream would be a key part of its meaning. I would see it as a strong confirmation of the fact that even though my spouse is physically dead, he still remains a vital part of my memory, my sense of self, my soul. The unusual intensity of the dream sensations dramatically underscores that fundamental truth—it's as if the dream were saying, "These feelings of your spouse are *real* and *true*, even though your waking consciousness thinks he is gone from your life forever." This, I think, is what dreams of the dead are ultimately getting at: reassuring people that even though death has physically separated them from their loved ones, they are still connected to their loved ones emotionally and spiritually, and they always will be.

Dan's dream seems to be serving exactly this function, in that his firefighter friend encourages him to accept the sorrowful reality of death and then renew his active commitment to life and to the work he and his friend shared. I suspect the emotional impact of the dream on Dan was greatly enhanced by the fact that the message of encouragement was delivered by this particular person, a close friend who gave his life to help others. Who else could give Dan as powerful a sense of consolation, reassurance, and

encouragement as his firefighter friend? I believe there is frequently a special meaning involved in the connection between the
messenger and the message in dreams of the dead, that is, a connection between the unique personal qualities of the deceased
loved one who appears in the dream and the particular content of
whatever he or she says to the dreamer.

A similar dream was experienced by Sam, the sixty-year-old
New Jersey man described in chapter 5, who used to work in the
World Trade Center towers, who knew hundreds of the people
who died, and who was having recurrent dreams after September
11 of burning skin sensations. He contacted me right after
Christmas to describe his strangest dream yet:

*On the night of 12/26/01, I awoke with the same prickly heat/burning
skin pain as before. I remembered having a dream about Douglas R. He
was a fellow I worked with at Cantor Fitzgerald and died on 9/11. My
wife, who works for a financial services company on Wall Street, created
a fundraising auction and raised several thousand dollars for his widow.
In the dream I dreamed that Douglas was aware of what my wife did
and was happy about it. What I don't understand is: If it was a good
dream and Douglas was happy about the situation, why was I having the
burning pain?[4]*

Like many other dreams of the dead, Sam's involves unusual
feelings and sensations that blur the line between dreaming and
waking experience. Sam's dream also conveys an ambivalent message, a disconcerting combination of painful despair and positive
reassurance that is similar to the dual message of Dan's dream. In
Sam's dream he becomes aware of the presence of his former
coworker Douglas, and he is specifically aware of Douglas's happiness regarding the moral and financial support Sam's wife has
provided to Douglas's widow. So a specific message of encouragement is conveyed by a person who is uniquely well suited to
deliver it, just like in Dan's dream. And also like Dan's dream,

Sam's combines an element of new vitality for the future with a painful reminder of the sorrows of the present. Sam asked why such a seemingly "good" dream would still include the burning sensation that has plagued him in several dreams since September 11. My reply was that this seems to be the way with dreams of the dead—they bring both lightness and darkness, both hope and despair, both a new opening to future growth and possibility and a painful reminder of the fears and frailties of the present. The task of the dreamer seems to be holding these opposing forces in conscious awareness and drawing wisdom, guidance, and energy from *both* of them.

Many other dreams that come in the aftermath of an unexpected disaster carry this same kind of dual emotional charge. Although such dreams may seem deeply perplexing and unsettling to the people who have them, I believe their value in the healing process lies precisely here, in offering an extraordinarily powerful *experience* of how seemingly antithetical emotions can be held together within the psyche. For people who have suffered a sudden tragedy, it may seem impossible ever to reconcile the intense emotions swirling within them, but that is exactly the role that dreams play in healing—by drawing on the deep symbolic power of the unconscious imagination, dreams envision that which *is* possible and that which *can* be achieved in waking consciousness.

This capacity of dreams to express and integrate a complex array of emotions in the form of striking images and sensations is beautifully illustrated in the experience of "Mandy," a twenty-nine-year-old artist from California. A couple of days before September 11, Mandy had flown to New York to visit her friend "Donna," who happened to work in one of the World Trade Center towers. On the morning of the eleventh Donna had gone to work as usual, leaving Mandy and another friend asleep in her apartment (right across the river from the towers), with plans to meet at the WTC for lunch. Mandy woke up right after the first plane hit, and this is what she said happened next:

> When we heard what was happening, and the TV and cell phones weren't working, we hopped on our bikes and rode down to the water to see what was going on. The second plane hit on our way there. Once we arrived at the waterfront, we watched the towers tumble to the ground. My main fear and worry was about my friend Donna. I found a pay phone and called her, but the only number I had was her work number, so I left a message on her voice mail. It was so bizarre, I was leaving a message in a place that had collapsed. It didn't make any sense....After the towers fell, we saw the smoke and ash hurtling toward us, like a big funnel cloud and that's when we rode home, getting covered in ash and dust on the ride home. It was so incredibly frightening. The sky was falling down on us and I couldn't see the sun. I really thought the world was ending for a few hours.[5]

It turned out her friend Donna was all right, although she had a harrowing escape down more than thirty flights of stairs, through dark clouds of smoke, and out into the frantic chaos of the streets. "She said the ground was littered with debris and high-heeled shoes, because all the ladies had to chuck them in order to run. What a surreal sight that must have been."[6] At the end of that awful day, when Mandy finally lay down to sleep, she prayed for a dream that might somehow salve the raw emotional wounds she had suffered. This is what came to her:

I'm walking through a forest that has been chopped down. It is a sea of stumps. Every single tree has been cut. I stand in the middle, sobbing. Who could do this? I walk up to one of the stumps and see the huge beau-

tiful spiral inside. I get lost in its magnificence. These trees are so old. I can see all of history in these trees, and I'm struck with the beauty and power of seeing this part of the tree. It's a part that I don't get to see. This spiral is taking me so deeply down into myself, to a place so powerful that it overwhelms me.[7]

Mandy said she got up the next morning with that same feeling of mysterious power carrying over into her waking awareness. She felt "so much calmer and clear-headed," and she said the beautiful image of the spiral helped her get through the agonies of the next day. Because she was a direct witness of the destruction of the WTC towers, Mandy's dream gives an especially clear illustration of how the dreaming imagination transforms waking events into metaphorical expressions. Mandy's dream is clearly related to the horrifying sights of that day, but her dream does not present those sights in a direct and literal fashion. Rather than showing the WTC towers collapsing, Mandy's dream portrays a forest whose trees have been cruelly and inexplicably chopped down. The symbolic connection between the towers and the trees is plainly evident, and yet what I think is most interesting is the way Mandy's dream goes beyond the obvious connections to explore important dimensions of the disaster that may not, in all the fear and frenzy of that day, have been fully appreciated by her conscious awareness. In her dream her attention is drawn not to the destruction of two very tall buildings, but to the wanton murder of a whole community of living beings. All her sadness and horror and confusion are focused on this desolate image of the razed forest; all the terrible emotions of the previous day find expression at this moment in the dream.

Then something new happens, something so powerful that it crosses over from the dream world into Mandy's waking awareness. As she is walking through the "sea of stumps" (an evocative phrase itself), she goes over to one of the stumps and sees "the huge beautiful spiral inside." Mandy realizes she's seeing something that is usually hidden from view, and she finds herself carried away with the ever-deepening movement of the spiral, all the way to a place of ancient power and overwhelming beauty. When she woke up, those positive, revitalizing dream feelings were still very much with her. To be sure, Mandy still felt scared and confused about what was going on in the waking world, but her dream had succeeded in bringing powerful new energies into her conscious awareness. If the trees had not been cut down, she never would have seen the beautiful spiral; if the terrorist attack had not occurred, she never would have needed to reach so far into her own psychospiritual depths. Out of tragedy comes hope; out of destruction, new life. This is the wisdom of our dreams.

Transformational Dream Analysis

Dreams of new hope for the future do not always come quickly to trauma survivors, and when they do occur they can easily be overlooked amid the repetitive nightmare themes of fear, misfortune, and vulnerability. But if trauma survivors and their caregivers pay close attention not just to the horrifying recurrent nightmares but also to the other, more "dreamlike" dreams that occur following the original disastrous event, they will often find surprising flashes of renewed vitality and the potential for healthy, creative living.

One method that can help in discerning these kinds of dreams is to use what I call "transformational dream analysis." It is a pretty simple method. You start by looking for the most common patterns, themes, and characters in a series of dreams.[8] Then, knowing what is most *common* in the dreams, you look for what is most *uncommon*—you look for singularities, for unique elements, for moments of special intensity and extraordinary bizarreness. You identify one particularly striking and impactful dream in the series, and you use it as a hermeneutic key to open new ways of understanding the series as a whole. I want to illustrate this method with the dreams of Nan we have been discussing in previous chapters. The dreams Nan experienced following her car accident offer a good case study of the healing dynamics of dreaming, and the approach I am using with her dreams can be used with anyone who has suffered a terrible crisis or disaster.

The first step of this method is to consider the most common themes, emotions, and characters in the dream series. In Nan's case, the results of this analysis are not surprising: Her dreams are filled with negative emotion, bodily misfortune (such as losing her sight), aggressive social interactions, and the disturbing presence of her ex-husband Phil. The second step is to use those common themes as means of highlighting what is uncommon and extraordinary in Nan's dreams. Is there a dream (or a small cluster of dreams) that really stands out from the others in terms of unusual content, intensity, bizarreness, and impact on the dreamer?

It is not always this easy, but in Nan's case there is a clear answer to that question. Her twentieth dream, which came almost six months after the accident, marks a striking departure from the recurrent themes that characterized her preceding dreams. Nan titled her twentieth post-trauma dream "I Painted My Room (Like Ziggy)":

20. *I'm in my bedroom at my parents home and I've decided to paint it. I go to Sarah [an admired art teacher] for advice and she shows me some very ordinary dusty blue fabric with a small wht or off wht pattern but she says she can't come help me yet; it will have to be later. I plan to wait on her but the next thing I know I am painting the walls of my room—all in one brush stroke I paint the walls in a bright and beautiful rainbow pattern! There is a space between 2 closet doors on one wall where I had planned to hang Sarah's fabric but I know now, it won't work. So I paint my own canvas to hang there in oranges and blues. Wow! Then I get some white clouds—I think I painted them on wood shaped like clouds—and hang them on the opposite long wall that is painted.*

When Sarah arrives she is amazed and says its beautiful and like no other.

This dream stands out dramatically from her other ones, for several reasons:

- In content terms, it is one of the very few positive dreams in the series (positive in having no misfortune, aggression, or negative emotion). Compared to the handful of other dreams without any negative elements, this one has more color, more positive evaluations, and more movement and volitional action.
- The dream revolves around Nan's possession of a magical object, the paintbrush that can paint a rainbow with a single stroke. This is the only instance in all her dreams in which Nan experiences what content analysis calls a "good fortune," that is, a beneficial occurrence not caused by the dreamer or another character. This is the only time in all of Nan's dreams where something good happens to her "out of the blue."
- "I Painted My Room (Like Ziggy)" is unique among Nan's dreams for its strong aesthetic qualities: the colors, the creativity, the beautiful painting of the rainbow, the appreciative reaction of the artist-teacher—amid the gloom, misfortune, and fearfulness of Nan's other dreams in the series, this one features her as a creator, an artist, a person with a surprising ability to bring new beauty into the world.

All of this evidence about the singularity of "I Painted My Room (Like Ziggy)" is based on a plain reading of the dreams, without knowing anything else about Nan. Now, when her personal associations are included, the full significance of this dream truly begins to emerge. Nan said the parenthetical title she gave the dream, "(like Ziggy)," was a reference to a children's book she used to enjoy reading with her children about a boy with a magic paintbrush. In the dream she has a paintbrush just like Ziggy's, one that can paint a rainbow at a single stroke. This reminder of her positive experiences in being a mother (she and Phil had four children) was matched by a reminder of her having worked throughout her life as a part-time art teacher in various elementary schools. The dream thus weaves together the two strongest historical threads of her identity (being a mother, being an art teacher). Coming at a time when Nan's identity is under siege— she is far from home and family, in training to start a brand new career, and suffering the physical and emotional after-effects of the accident—this dream had the effect of "re-minding" Nan of talents, strengths, and resources within her that have survived the trauma and are available to help her through this time of crisis and transition.

When I spoke to Nan about her dreams, she herself singled out this one for special consideration. She said the mention of painting clouds was especially significant to her because it immediately reminded her of a time when Phil had brought her to a very famous and high-priced therapist for marriage counseling. Phil complained to the therapist that Nan's head was "up in the clouds," and to his surprise the therapist replied that perhaps Nan was there because that is where God is. Ever since, Nan has felt a happy spiritual kinship with clouds, and their presence in this dream greatly enhanced its meaning for her.

When Nan was asked when exactly the dream occurred, she checked her journal and experienced a very strong "Aha!" sensation: The dream came on March 31, Easter Sunday. Her life had been so upside-down for so long, Nan had not even noticed that the dream came on what is for many Christians the holiest day of the religious year. When Nan made the connection between the date and her dream, it didn't change her view of the dream's meaning so much as tremendously deepened its impact on her, adding a whole new symbolic dimension of sacrifice, death, and resurrection. For a person training for the ministry, having a powerful dream on Easter Sunday about a rainbow (the sign of God's covenant to Noah after the world-destroying flood) is about as religiously charged an experience as one could imagine. For Nan, the dream was a divine gift she was only just beginning to understand and appreciate.

Let me turn to the third step of my method, which is to ask what this most unusual dream can tell us about the series of dreams as a whole. Right off, I believe her "I Painted My Room (Like Ziggy)" is a clear sign of Nan's success in overcoming the worst effects of the car accident. It is a striking contrast to her first dream, where she is a frightened, passive observer of the threatening curtains in her hospital room; here she is actively creating a new space in a familiar, "homey" setting. It is also a striking contrast to her fourth dream, with the young woman lying in the white shower; in her twentieth dream Nan brings vibrant color back into her life, countering the image in her fourth dream of the young woman's life draining away in a stream of faint pink. (Nan associated the young woman's bleeding with a first menstruation—the initiation of a woman's procreative life.)

A special focus on "I Painted My Room (Like Ziggy)" also reveals a new dimension to her dream struggles with her ex-husband Phil. We have already discussed (chapter 6) the frequent appearance of Phil in Nan's dreams following her accident, and if we look now at her Phil dreams in relation to "I Painted My Room (Like Ziggy)," it is interesting to note that in three of her Phil dreams before this one Nan passively accepts Phil's superior status and her inability to do anything about "his insertion into my life," while in the two Phil dreams that came after her twentieth one she angrily fights back against him and actively (though still vainly) tries to end his power over her. I suggest that "I

Painted My Room (Like Ziggy)," with its "anti-Phil" image of the clouds, is further evidence for the idea we proposed earlier about the significance of Phil in all these dreams: His presence is a metaphorical expression of Nan's feelings of weakness, vulnerability, and dependence following the accident. Since their divorce thirteen years earlier, Nan had successfully begun a new life for herself—but suddenly the car crash threatened everything in her world, throwing her back into a situation of helpless dependence. The frequency of the Phil dreams shows that a vital task in Nan's process of healing from her trauma is to regain her cherished sense of independence and personal integrity. The fact that the most emotionally intense Phil dreams come *after* the psychologically and spiritually empowering experience of the "I Painted My Room (Like Ziggy)" dream is, I believe, a positive sign of her resurgent strength and her willingness to confront the tough issues that lie ahead.

That may sound paradoxical—the healthier Nan becomes, the more she dreams about her problems—but it actually reflects the potent healing power of the dreaming imagination. Although we may wish it were otherwise, dreaming can never make our waking-world problems disappear. However, dreaming does serve the extremely valuable function of rallying our emotional strength in times of crisis and focusing our energies on the best available options for overcoming our waking difficulties. In Nan's nightmares the seeds of new hope are taking root and starting to grow once again, and that is cause for rejoicing and thanksgiving whatever may come in her future.

A Conversation with Reverend Coughlin

Over the years, as I have talked with different people about their dreams, reflected on my own dreams, and studied a variety of theories about the nature and function of dreaming, I have developed an ever-increasing appreciation for the power of dreams to expand, enrich, and stimulate growth in human consciousness. More than that, I have come to believe that the transformative powers of dreaming can promote not only the growth of individuals but of whole communities as well. I know, of course, that many people in contemporary Western society have trouble accepting the idea that dreams have any value at all, so the suggestion that dreams can contribute to the welfare of the broader community is bound to seem absurd. Nevertheless, this is my hope, which has become all the stronger after the horrors of September 11: That everyone tries to pay just a little more attention to their dreams, as a means of understanding more clearly the unconscious fears, wishes, and aspirations that motivate our interactions with each other. Although greater public dream awareness would not magically solve all global problems, I believe it would provide valuable insights into our relations with people different from ourselves, and it would provide an unconscious "reality check" on our waking-world efforts to overcome large-scale social conflicts.

I raised this issue in a conversation I had with the Reverend Dan Coughlin, the Chaplain of the U.S. House of Representatives.[9] We spoke in early November, and I told him I was curious to know how our government leaders were coping with the emotional aftershocks of September 11. I especially wanted to know (though I was pretty sure I already knew the answer) whether anyone in Congress ever talked about their dreams in relation to politics, their personal lives, or anything else. Rev. Coughlin was quite generous and friendly in his response to my questions. He had been in Washington for a year and a half, and he said he found the representatives to be more religiously devoted than he had originally expected. Many of them were motivated by their religious faith to pursue politics, and while in Washington they maintained an active engagement in prayer,

Bible study, and worship. Rev. Coughlin commented on the tremendous stress felt by many representatives in their family relations. He said Congress was just like the rest of corporate America in requiring long hours, frequent travel, and immediate response to unexpected emergencies. In this regard he compared the religious activities of many representatives to the involvement of other representatives in various support and stress management groups. After September 11, Rev. Coughlin was quietly approached by many House members who were deeply troubled by the terrorist attack (which had of course targeted Washington in addition to New York City). What surprised Rev. Coughlin was that the representatives were asking for his help not just for their own religious needs, but also for their urgent political efforts to understand better the religions of *other* people. The representatives realized that one crucial dimension of the terrorist attack involved a violent historical quarrel between Judaism, Christianity, and Islam, and they turned to Rev. Coughlin for insight into the different beliefs and attitudes that have generated such hatred among the three religious traditions.

When I asked Rev. Coughlin directly whether anyone in Congress ever spoke about their dreams, he gave the answer I was expecting: No, he had never heard of any dream conversations among the House members. He could not say for sure why this was, though he suspected it was due in part to the negative publicity First Lady Nancy Reagan received when her interests in astrology were revealed back in the 1980s. No politician would want to subject him or herself to that kind of embarrassing public ridicule, and that made it unlikely that anyone would voluntarily share something as seemingly irrational and bizarre as a dream. "Even significant dreams you wouldn't hear about," Rev. Coughlin commented. However, he did say that some representatives spoke periodically of their "daydreams," by which he meant their ideals, their hopes, and their visions of a better world.

193

Rev. Coughlin noted that staff members working in Congress were especially likely to talk about their daydreams in this sense, and he expressed amazement at how many congressional staffers were motivated to come to Washington by a deep passion for community service. Unfortunately, he saw far too many staffers become bitterly disillusioned by the petty infighting of Washington officialdom, and as a result "the dreams get tainted."

As I spoke with Rev. Coughlin, it became clear that the great challenge for those people who run our government (staffers and leaders alike) is to stay true to their deepest, most cherished ideals despite the relentless challenges, seductive temptations, and painful difficulties involved in the day-to-day practice of their jobs. I was heartened to hear about the importance they attribute to their "daydreams," although I felt terribly distressed at the idea that people who work in Washington are so guarded about their inner lives that they can't talk about their "night dreams." That suggests to me an atmosphere of such insecurity, anxiety, and interpersonal menace that I truly wonder how anyone in Washington can function in a psychologically and spiritually healthy way.

My conversation with Rev. Coughlin confirmed my feeling that any effort to promote greater public awareness of dreaming was unlikely to receive support or encouragement from our governmental leaders (although I still enjoy imagining the president, congressional leaders, and Supreme Court Justices all getting together to share their dreams, talk honestly about their personal projections, and reflect together on creative new approaches to the country's biggest problems). I know that, for better or for worse, the impetus for greater public dream awareness is going to have to come from people outside the official spheres of power, people whose dreaming imaginations will give voice to the fears, hopes, and desires of the whole community. My hope ultimately rests with them.

Essential Bibliography

Bulkeley, Kelly. 1995. *Spiritual Dreaming: A Cross-Cultural and Historical Journey*. Mahwah: Paulist Press.

Domhoff, G. William. 1996. *Finding Meaning in Dreams: A Quantitative Approach*. New York: Plenum.

Hall, Calvin, & Robert Van de Castle. 1966. *The Content Analysis of Dreams*. New York: Appleton-Century-Crofts.

Night Terrors: Trauma Can Spark Nightmares—and Also Aid Healing. 2001. *New York Newsday*, 10/10.

Notes

1. Night Terrors 2001.
2. Night Terrors 2001.
3. See Bulkeley 1995.
4. Personal communication, 1/1/02.
5. Personal communication, 10/19/01.
6. Personal communication, 10/19/01.
7. Personal communication, 9/18/01.
8. This is what the Hall and Van de Castle system of content analysis is best at providing. See Domhoff 1996; Hall & Van de Castle 1966.
9. I thank my uncle-in-law Tom Campbell for putting me in touch with Rev. Coughlin.

Conclusion

The Practice of Dreamsharing

The practice of dreamsharing is like the practice of anything else—
the best way to learn about it is by *doing* it. Nothing I can tell you
in this book will teach you as much about dreamsharing as will
actually talking with people about dreams. And of course, I heartily
encourage you to go out and do just that. Whatever else I have said
in the preceding chapters, I hope readers will have gained a clear
sense of how surprisingly accessible dreamsharing can be. The
ability to discuss dreams and derive insight from them requires no
special training, advanced education, or professional expertise.
Anyone can do this—the basic practice of dreamsharing is open to
anyone who is willing to make an honest, open-minded go of it.
Humans have been talking with each other about their dreams for
thousands and thousands of years; all of us have a natural capacity
to engage in this universal mode of interpersonal communication.
While I very much appreciate the work of skilled mental health
professionals (particularly in times of severe collective crisis), I am
emphatically opposed to any attempt to restrict dreamsharing to a
psychotherapeutic context. People who are suffering acute mental
distress should definitely seek the help of professionals, but people
who want to talk with someone about their dreams should feel free
to consult anyone, professional or otherwise, who can listen well,
is open to new meanings, and will respect their confidence.

The various techniques I have described in the preceding
chapters can be summarized and condensed into the form of a

brief dreamsharing protocol. What follows is the sequence of steps I generally use in dreamsharing with both individuals and groups. I use the same approach, with a few changes of wording, in dreamsharing with children as well as with adults. Everyone who works with dreams for long enough develops their own distinctive way of guiding the process, so I offer this protocol not as the final word on dream interpretation but rather as a point of reference to help you work out an approach that is comfortable and right for you.

A Dreamsharing Protocol

- Start by asking the dreamer to describe the dream, in as much detail as possible, using the present tense.
- Ask questions of clarification about particular elements of the dream (for example, asking for more descriptive details about the setting, characters, colors, emotions, and so on). Invite the dreamer to recreate in waking consciousness the feelings, images, and moods of the dream, as vividly as possible (including bodily sensations).
- Reflect on your own initial projections, and if appropriate share them with the dreamer, using the "If it were my dream..." preface.
- Ask for associations to the different elements of the dream (for example, questions about waking-life connections to the setting, characters, colors, emotions, and so on). Invite the dreamer to try bridging the dream to the waking world, taking the dream as a possible metaphorical expression of something going on in the dreamer's current life.
- Identify the point (or points) in the dream of greatest tension, energy, and vividness. Invite the dreamer to sit for a

moment with that part of the dream and see what feelings or ideas come from it.

- Discuss potential ways of carrying the dream's energy into the waking world (for example, through artistic creativity, private symbolic gestures, shifts in belief or behavior, or starting new projects). Invite the dreamer to consider the question, "Where can I *go* with this dream?"

- When the time has come to bring things to a close, end by reflecting (humbly) on the many questions left unanswered and the many loose threads of meaning still hanging from the dream. Invite the dreamer to think of what he or she would most like to learn from a future dream.

That's all there is to it. Each of these steps can be refined and expanded, of course, and I encourage readers to experiment with different techniques to see which ones work best in which situations. The most effective dream interpreters are those people who have built up through long experience a good sense of judgment about how to approach different kinds of dreams and different kinds of dreamers. This sense of judgment that comes from dreamsharing is a remarkable thing. I have found that over a long enough period of time, most people who practice dreamsharing develop an unusual kind of symbolic wisdom that can be fruitfully applied in realms outside of dream interpretation (for example, in teaching, art, health care, community work, cultural criticism, and such endeavors). This is perhaps the greatest practical benefit of dreamsharing, and it is the main reason why I believe dreamsharing should not be confined to the psychotherapy office but should be encouraged much more broadly as a natural, healthful means of emotional communication in homes, schools, places of worship, and even places of work.

The Theory of Dreamsharing

In addition to summarizing the practical techniques of dreamsharing, I want to pull together the various strands of our discussion about current theorizing in the study of dreams. Can dreamsharing with people who have suffered a severe crisis tell us anything about the general nature and function of dreaming? Surprisingly, both Freud and Jung answered this question with an evasive "No." Late in his career Freud decided that dreams from soldiers suffering "war neuroses" could not be explained as instinctual wish fulfillments, but rather reflected the efforts of the ego to master the waking-life trauma.[1] Jung called them "pure reaction-dreams" and set them apart from the rest of his theory, saying "a dream of this kind, which is essentially only a reproduction of the trauma, can hardly be called compensatory."[2] Although Freud and Jung disagreed on many things, they essentially agreed on this point, that dreams following a trauma are insignificant exceptions to a general theory of dream functioning.

Undeterred by Freud's and Jung's disinterest in these types of dreams, many of today's leading researchers (including Ernest Hartmann, Deirdre Barrett, and G. William Domhoff) have taken post-traumatic nightmares as the key phenomenon in their understanding of the formation and function of dreaming. These researchers center their thinking on the finding that many victims of PTSD experience a progression from repetitive nightmares of the traumatizing event to more "normal" dreams in which the event is woven into other life concerns. For Hartmann, this highlights the way dreaming "makes connections" in the mind.[3] For Barrett, this illustrates the therapeutic value of dreamsharing in the professional treatment of trauma survivors.[4] For Domhoff, this is clear evidence of the "repetition dimension," by which dreaming reflects "a preoccupation with problems we have not resolved."[5] In each case, post-traumatic dreams are taken as unusually pure expressions of the basic processes underlying all types of dreaming.

I have raised several objections to this mainstream view of PTSD nightmares as an adequate paradigm for a general theory of dreaming. First of all, health is not the lack of pathology. Researchers who use a pathological condition like post-traumatic nightmares as a paradigm to generalize about the functions of the dreaming imagination in a healthy condition are following a dead-end path. Healthy human functioning has dynamic qualities of its own, and this makes it logically fallacious to claim that knowledge of psychopathology can provide a wholly adequate model of psychological health. As important as it is to study post-traumatic nightmares, any attempt to privilege the theoretical significance of these kinds of dreams is unwarranted and misguided.

Second, I agree with Hartmann and others who see crisis dreams as efforts to contextualize the traumatizing experience and make sense of it in connection with the rest of the person's world. However, I question the conservative tone of this emphasis on connections, and I question the pervasive use in the clinical literature on PTSD of words like *mastery, control, normalize,* and *balance.* Dreams following a crisis do not aim at simply making the person "normal" again, with no other goal than restoring the emotional *status quo ante*—rather, they aim at the development of a whole new understanding of self and world that is slowly created out of the broken ruins of the dreamer's pre-trauma self. The mainstream view of PTSD sounds to me like all the king's horses and all the king's men claiming they have put Humpty Dumpty together again. I do not think people who have experienced a severe crisis can ever be "put together again" in quite the same way as they were before, and I believe the ultimate function of their dreams is to help them find radically new kinds of meaning, hope, and structure in the world.

Third, dreaming has both personal and collective dimensions. Many psychologists regard dreams as nothing more than reflections of the individual's private fears, wishes, and concerns. This is true for most dreams. But this common psychological assumption neglects the fact that some dreams also have collective dimensions that speak to the fears, wishes, and concerns of the dreamer's community (a fact that is recognized by a majority of the world's non-Western cultural traditions). The dreams people experience following a severe trauma often include elements of both personal and collective significance, and any interpretive approach that fails to account for these multiple levels of meaning cannot provide a wholly adequate explanation of dreaming (even if an exclusive focus on the personal dimension may, as a practical matter, be therapeutically effective).

For these and other reasons, I cannot agree with researchers who claim PTSD nightmares are the key to understanding the formation and function of dreams. I would use a different metaphor and say that studying dreams of crisis is one good pathway into the realm of dreaming—it is not the only pathway into that mysterious wilderness, but it is a good one, and it reveals certain features of the terrain better than other pathways (even as those other pathways reveal features that are completely ignored by this one). My point is that a full theoretical mapping of the realm of dreaming cannot be achieved by following one path alone. Such a mapping requires an integration of information from several different paths, and contemporary dream researchers have only just begun this process. Indeed, few researchers have any familiarity with the work being done by people outside their field of specialization, and this has led to a great deal of needless cross-talking, confusion over terminology, and old-fashioned turf battles. Strong institutional forces work against integrative, interdisciplinary thinking, and fighting against these forces is a major challenge for all dream researchers.

The limitations of our current theoretical knowledge should not, however, be taken as cause for despair. On the contrary, this is a very exciting time for the study of dreams, as recent developments in cognitive neuroscience, religious studies, anthropology, and computer technology have given researchers tremendous new abilities to expand the range, sophistication, and interdisciplinary quality of their investigations. No one can predict where these investigations will lead or what exactly will be discovered, but we can be sure that whatever comes from the work of dream researchers over the next ten to twenty years, it will enhance and enrich our understanding of the nature and destiny of human existence.

Dreams of the Future

America's most immediate response to the terrorist attack of September 11 took a military form: we attacked the Taliban and Al Qaeda forces in Afghanistan, increased the presence of armed troops in our public spaces, and allocated billions of dollars for new weapons and improved intelligence gathering. However, as necessary and reassuring as these steps may have been, we cannot allow them to be our only response to the events of September 11. Military action by itself will never be sufficient to prevent future terrorist attacks. Missiles, tanks, and rifles cannot create a world that is free from hatred and violence. To make real progress toward that goal, we need new insights into our troubled relations with people from different religions and cultural traditions. We need to understand better the fears, hopes, and desires motivating our behavior in the world and the behavior of those we fight against. We need creative visions of new social relations and new forms of communal interaction. We need to combine forceful action with deep, sustained reflection. Although we have rightly focused much of our attention on military matters, the time has surely come for us to attend to the more contemplative process of reflecting on our horrifying experiences and creating new meaning out of the shattered fragments of our pre–September 11 world.

This, I suggest to you, is the fundamental challenge for caregivers during any kind of crisis, and it is a task that may be greatly aided by an understanding of dreams and nightmares. Dreaming is one of the most powerful sources of meaning-making in our lives. Whether it is considered a naturally evolved, hard-wired function of the human brain or a sacred portal of divine guidance and inspiration (I see it as both), dreaming creatively integrates our experiences of self and world and helps sustain our adaptive vitality in daily life. Particularly in times of sudden disaster or unexpected crisis, when we feel overwhelmed with confusion, fear, and despair, dreams work to revive our energies, reorient our emotions, and reinvigorate our hopes for the future.

In the end, healing is a mystery. What is it that enables a person to move from suffering and despair to a renewed capacity for creative living? Can anyone say they know for sure? I can't. But that's all right, because I know from experience that the practice of dreamsharing can actively promote the mysterious energies of healing to greater effectiveness. I hope I have persuaded you to give this practice a try, so you can discover for yourself the healing powers of dreaming.

Essential Bibliography

Barrett, Deirdre, ed. 1996. *Trauma and Dreams.* Cambridge: Harvard University Press.

Bulkeley, Kelly. 1997. *An Introduction to the Psychology of Dreaming.* Westport: Praeger.

Domhoff, G. William. 1996. *Finding Meaning in Dreams: A Quantitative Approach.* New York: Plenum.

Hartmann, Ernest. 1995. Making Connections in a Safe Place: Is Dreaming Psychotherapy? *Dreaming* 5 (4):213–28.

Jung, C. G. 1974. General Aspects of Dream Psychology. In *Dreams*. Princeton: Princeton University Press.

Notes

1. Bulkeley 1997, 22–23.
2. Jung 1974, 46–47.
3. Hartmann 1995.
4. Barrett 1996.
5. Domhoff 1996, 194.

Index